hot for food
all day

LAUREN TOYOTA

hot for food
all day

easy recipes to level up
your *vegan* meals

TEN SPEED PRESS
California | New York

CONTENTS

INTRODUCTION   1

INGREDIENTS & STUFF   3

STUFF YOU NEED   7

BREAKFAST STUFF   13

Tofu Scramble   14

Mung Bean Scramble   17

   LEVEL UP!

   Mushroom Kimchi Omelet   18

   Breakfast Za   20

   Breakfast Totchos   23

   Stuffed Breakfast Danishes   24

Two Potato Rösti   26

Scones 4 Ways   28

   Sundried Tomato,
Olive & Chive Scones   30

   Jalapeño Cheddar Scones   30

   Strawberry Cardamom Scones   30

   Blueberry Lemon Scones   30

   Tahini Glaze   31

   LEVEL UP!

   Savory Broken Scone
Breakfast Muffins   32

Baked Peanut Butter & Jam Oat Bars   35

Apple Crumble Muffins   36

Crunchy Coconut Granola   39

My Blender Juice 3 Ways   41

   Real Green Juice   41

   Sunny Citrus Juice   41

   Immune Warrior Juice   41

My Fave Smoothie   43

LUNCH STUFF   45

Tortilla Soup   46

   LEVEL UP!

   Red Sauce Enchiladas   48

   Chipotle Cheese Fries   51

Creamy Green Pea Soup   52

   LEVEL UP!

   Creamy Green Pea Soup with   55
   Pasta & Parmesan

Corn Chowder   56

   LEVEL UP!

   Cacio e Pepe   58

   Corn Chowder Hollandaise   60

Zuppa Toscana   62

Clubhouse Sandwich   66

Spicy Lentil Wrap   69

Fried Artichoke Sandwich   70

My Everyday Sandwich   75

My Everyday Roasted Vegetable Salad   76

   LEVEL UP!

   Roasted Vegetable Potstickers   78

Fries & Salad   80

THE BOWL BIBLE   82

Grain Bases   84

Cooked Veg   86

     Grilled Romaine Hearts   88

     Roasted Purple Cabbage Slaw   88

     Steamed Kale, Bok Choy & Broccoli   89

     Blistered Tomatoes   89

     Roasted Curry Cauliflower   89

Hearty Additions   90

     Crispy Tofu Fingers   92

     Miso-Roasted Kabocha Squash   95

     Crunchy Butter Beans   96

     Chicken Shawarma   99

     Tempeh Bacon Chunks   100

Grilled Cheese 4 Ways   102

     The "Sharp" Grilled Cheese   104

     LEVEL UP!

     The "Spiced" Grilled Cheese   105

     The "Sweet" Grilled Cheese   106

     The "Creamy" Grilled Cheese   107

DINNER STUFF   109

One-Pot Mac n' Cheese   110

     LEVEL UP!

     Buffalo Chicken Mac n' Cheese   113

     Pizza Mac n' Cheese   115

     Thai Red Curry Mac n' Cheese   116

     Tex-Mex Mac n' Cheese   119

     Green Mac n' Cheese   120

Ragu Bolognese   122

Easy Brussels Sprouts Pasta   124

     LEVEL UP!

     Bacon Kale Pasta   127

Easy Tofu & Veggie Stir-Fry   128

Miso-Roasted Kabocha Squash 3 Ways   130

     LEVEL UP!

     Kabocha Stuffed Shells   130

     Kabocha Wonton Ravioli with Miso Butter   132

     Kabocha Broth with Udon   135

Cauliflower Steaks 2 Ways, with Spaghetti Aglio e Olio (Piccata & Parm)   136

     LEVEL UP!

     Korean BBQ Burritos   140

Buffalo Chicken Crunch Wraps   142

Sloppy Joe Zucchini Boats   145

     LEVEL UP!

     Zucchini Carbonara   146

Crispy Tofu Fingers 2 Ways   150

     LEVEL UP!

     Charred Corn Salad   150

     HFF Famous Bowls   153

     LEVEL UP!

Mushroom Kraut Potato Cakes   154

SNACKS, STAPLES & SAUCY STUFF 157

LEVEL UP!
Butter Chicken Nachos 159

All-Green Fresh Rolls with
Green Curry Dipping Sauce 160

Classic Onion Dip 163

LEVEL UP!
Stuffed Potato Skins with Onion Dip 164

Blistered Shishito Peppers 167

LEVEL UP!
Blistered Shishito Peppers
with Ramen 168

Warm Shishito Pepper Dip 173

Smoky Cheese Spread 174

LEVEL UP!
Savory Cheese Tart 177

HFF Snack Mixes 5 Ways 178

Homemade Stove-Top Popcorn 180

Everything Bagel Popcorn Seasoning
+ Snack Mix 181

Dill Pickle Popcorn Seasoning
+ Snack Mix 181

Tokyo Mix Popcorn Seasoning
+ Snack Mix 182

Old Bay Popcorn Seasoning
+ Snack Mix 182

Pink Beet Caramel Popcorn
+ Snack Mix 183

LEVEL UP!
Tokyo Street Fries 185

Sweet & Sour Rice Balls 186

Egg Yolk Sauce 188

Cilantro Sour Cream 189

Jalapeño Ranch 190

Gochujang Aioli 191

Sesame Ginger Sauce 192

Pumpkin Miso Gravy 193

Crispy Onion Strings 194

Old Bay Croutons 197

Salad Dressings for Dummies 198

Tahini Caesar Dressing 200

Pink Goddess Dressing 200

Sesame Soy Vinaigrette 201

Creamy Pesto Dressing 201

Use Up the Hummus Dressing 201

SWEET STUFF 203

LEVEL UP!

Rocky Road Bars 205

Chocolate Chip Corn Cookies 206

Snickledoodles 209

Coconut Pecan Biscotti 210

Doughnut Holes 3 Ways 212

Loaf Cakes 3 Ways 214

    Lemon Chia Seed Loaf Cake 214

    Black Forest Loaf Cake 216

    Pumpkin Loaf Cake 219

Chocolate Peanut Butter Krispie Cake 222

Passion Fruit Slice 225

No-Churn Salted Caramel Tahini
Ice Cream 226

    LEVEL UP!

    Salted Caramel Tahini Milkshake 229

Puff Pastry 4 Ways 230

    Pumpkin Cheesecake Pinwheels 232

    Mini Strawberry Tarts 233

    Stone Fruit Galette 234

    Chocolate Almond Crescent Rolls 235

ABOUT THE AUTHOR 239

ACKNOWLEDGMENTS 240

INDEX 242

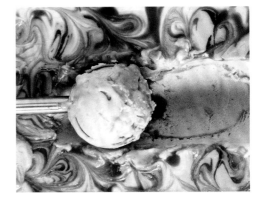

introduction

WELL, HERE WE ARE AGAIN, MY FRIENDS. I really couldn't do this without you and your enthusiasm for hot for food and the vegan food I make. In fact, it's SO moving that I wanted to put myself through the madness of making a second cookbook because of it. Thanks for waiting, and thank you for supporting my endeavors in a way that makes me want to ugly cry on the floor!

This cookbook is a companion piece to *Vegan Comfort Classics* in that I want you to treat my cookbooks like your vegan bibles. Everything you could ever want and imagine and maybe didn't even know you needed in your life is contained in the pages of these cookbooks. While the first book gave you a great foundation, this book is going to round out your arsenal of classic comfort foods. That means it is packed with some super simple go-to's and easy everyday stuff that I whip up quick in my kitchen, including some things you can prep and plan in advance if you're into that kind of thing. And don't worry, there are still some stand-out, unique, V-hot for food kinds of recipes that you'll definitely want to show off to your unconverted friends and fam.

One thing I focus on sharing more in this book is my knack for reusing, repurposing, and transforming leftovers and remnants of recipes into brand-new eats ('cause leftovers suck). That's right: I found a way to bring the *RECIPE?!* to life in print. If you've been following the hot for food journey thus far, ya already know what a *RECIPE?!* is. But if you're new here, I'll give you the lowdown.

A *RECIPE?!* isn't really a formal recipe but a rough, adaptable blueprint. When testing and developing delicious stuff, I have to make things up as I go and then do it again to finesse the amounts and tweak things so they're perfect. It's all very intuitive, so I try to encourage this kind of thing for anyone because it's how one really learns *how* to cook. And because I'm a recipe developer, I always have bits and pieces of recipes in my fridge including extra fillings, sauces, and so forth that I don't want to throw out. So I use everything up and make up my own meals with whatever I have on hand when I'm hungry. I managed to document this ridiculous but highly entertaining and educational process on video and put it on my YouTube channel, which quickly became a hit! It was the *realness* and achievable nature of cooking that I guess everyone liked. It's certainly how I like cooking on camera because I don't need to perfect anything before shooting. I just waltz into the kitchen and take out stuff in my fridge and pantry, cook in real time, and pray it'll turn out to be tasty. It usually is, thankfully!

In this cookbook you'll see that I've taken some of those long-lost ideas and *RECIPE?!* home runs and perfected them for you, giving you inspiration for using up whatever you have on hand. On top of that, I also figured out ways y'all are gonna level up your leftovers into brand-new meals using the stuff you make in this book. Throughout the cookbook, look for *LEVEL UP!* in the top corner to identify the recipes that are made from leftovers. Before you can level up, ya gotta backtrack to the page where the master recipe lives. You'll get the hang of it in no time.

You'll also see throughout the chapters some fun menu plans of stuff to eat on various occasions, like stuff to bring to a BYOVD (bring your own vegan dish) event! There's some inspo from stuff I eat when I'm busy, or when I'm Netflix-and-chillin' on a Sunday. It's endless food porn so you can stay hot for food all day! You're going to gasp over my **Sweet & Sour Rice Balls (page 186)**, **Butter Chicken Nachos (page 159)**, and **Stuffed Breakfast Danishes (page 24)**. I even concocted a new-and-improved vegan mac n' cheese that's made in one pot (page 110) PLUS there're five ways to level up the flavor! Did someone say **Thai Red Curry Mac n' Cheese (page 116)**? And as per usual, my love of baking took over for dessert stuff. I've got luscious loaf cake recipes x 3 (page 214), some easy ways to use more frozen vegan puff pastry (page 230) in your life, and an incredible **No-Churn Salted Caramel Tahini Ice Cream (page 226)** to share with you.

So with all that said, I'm just asking you to keep my *RECIPE?!* ethos in mind at all times. You don't have to follow the rules because there are none! Dive into this cookbook trusting that each and every meal you create for yourself is going to be delectable and delicious and just happens to be made from plants. I want you to take my ideas and try them but also use them as stepping-stones to start working your own wizardry. Tap into that kitchen intuition. Play around, mix and match, use what you have if you don't have what I listed, and just make it work!

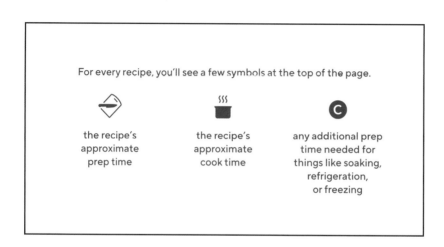

For every recipe, you'll see a few symbols at the top of the page.

| the recipe's approximate prep time | the recipe's approximate cook time | any additional prep time needed for things like soaking, refrigeration, or freezing |

ingredients & stuff

First let's quickly go over some basics about the ingredients you'll see in this cookbook. I get asked questions all the time about these staples, which are listed in order of importance to *ME*.

Oil. I'm not oil free…obviously. Oil brings flavor and fat to great cooking and that's that. *Neutral vegetable oil* means to use an oil with a high smoke point like *canola*, *safflower*, *sunflower*, *grapeseed*, *corn*, or *peanut*. It's light yellow in color, will be fairly inexpensive, and comes in a larger bottle. I wouldn't use this oil for dressings, but you can use it for most anything else in the cookbook that requires sautéing, shallow frying, baking, or roasting. This category also includes *avocado oil*, which is safe for high heat as well and is also neutral in flavor. It's become my go-to cooking oil when sautéing and using only a couple of tablespoons. That said, when deep frying, stick to the first options I mentioned, as they're less expensive, and do not use *coconut oil* or *olive oil*.

When I list *olive oil*, I mean a light olive oil that isn't cold pressed and isn't labeled extra virgin. I use it for other medium-heat sautéing or roasting, such as in stir-fries, soups, roasted vegetables, and so on. *Extra-virgin olive oil* should really be used as a finishing oil, so for dressings or for drizzling to finish a pasta. Same idea with *toasted sesame oil*, but sometimes I cook with a small amount of that one. You can also sauté or roast with *coconut oil* (virgin tastes like coconut and refined doesn't—refined also has a higher heat threshold). I decide between using an olive oil versus coconut oil depending on the flavor of the finished dish: Do I want to have the taste of olive oil in it? For **Zuppa Toscana (page 62)**, **Cauliflower Piccata & Parm (page 136)**, and anything Italian or European inspired, olive oil is great. The reason I use coconut oil is sometimes for the taste but also because it can usually be substituted for *vegan butter* because it's solid when cold. Speaking of, I really like *vegan butter sticks* for baking, and now you can find multiple brands that all vary slightly in taste and texture. These are made with a blend of cold-pressed vegetable oils and are an exact 1:1 sub for dairy butter.

Sugar. I'm also not sugar free. Well-balanced recipes, flavor profiles, and goddamn indulgent desserts need sugar. Sugar is vegan, contrary to some ridiculous Internet articles. However, some brands of refined sugar (granulated sugar, brown sugar, and confectioners' sugar) may still use animal bone char to filter and refine the sugar. In Canada (where I'm from), Redpath Sugar does nothing of the sort. Other than that, generally the organic brands don't use bone char. Demerara, turbinado, coconut sugar, and molasses are not refined so there's nothing to worry about there. You can also check manufacturers' FAQs online or contact them to find the info you need. When I mention *granulated sugar* in the ingredients, I'm being generic. I usually use a fine granulated cane sugar, but you can also use white refined granulated sugar. In general, do not substitute large amounts of granulated sugar for brown sugar in baked goods or it will alter the final results.

Stock. This means vegetable stock or broth. But my fave is using a vegan chicken-flavored or beef-flavored bouillon base/paste or bouillon cubes. I usually find these at specialty health-food stores, or you can order them online. In my recipes where I use these for liquid stock, there will be instructions for how much bouillon base to use per cup of water. In some cases, I use the bouillon base straight up with other seasonings, so if you can only get cubes, dissolve the cube in a little bit of warm water to make a paste. Now, if you can't find these meat-flavored stock options, substitute them for the same volume of liquid with a vegetable or mushroom stock or use vegetable, mushroom, or onion bouillon cubes. For soups you'll always adjust sea salt at the end to YOUR taste. No store-bought stock/broth is the same when it comes to sodium, flavor, or color, so results will vary slightly.

Thickeners and binders. You'll see things listed like cornstarch, tapioca flour (same as starch), and arrowroot flour (same as starch). There's a reason I use one over the other, so only use substitutes if I mention that you can in the ingredients list for the recipe; otherwise your results will not be the same.

Coconut cream and coconut milk. There is a difference between these two. Because they are different I always have the two on hand! I started seeing cans of coconut cream a few years ago, but they're not as common everywhere. Coconut cream has far less water or milk in the cans than full-fat coconut milk, but it still has some. If a recipe calls for canned coconut cream it means you only want to use the thick cream that usually separates from any liquid in a can of coconut milk, or you can search for cans labeled *coconut cream*. I've specified if a recipe benefits from having no liquid at all or if a little bit in the mix is OK. If you can't find canned coconut cream then canned full-fat coconut milk will suffice, but in some recipes you'll need more than one can to make up the total amount of coconut cream required. If using canned full-fat coconut milk, it's usually easiest if you put the can in the fridge for a few days before using; this will help separate the liquid from the cream, making it easier to scoop out the coconut cream.

Kala namak. You might be unfamiliar with this ingredient, also known as Himalayan black salt. Its sulfurous smell and taste lends itself to scrambles, the **Egg Yolk Sauce (page 188)**, and other savory applications. It's typically used in South Asia, but if you want to add it to your pantry, you'll find it in larger spice shops or at Indian or Asian grocers, or you can order it online. It's definitely optional in the few recipes where I used it in this cookbook, but if you buy it once, it'll last forever and you'll find yourself throwing a pinch into things the more you become accustomed to it.

Vegan convenience products. We've come a LONG way with vegan convenience products, and it makes ME joyful! We've even come a long way since I developed *Vegan Comfort Classics* in terms of ingenuity, availability, and diversity of vegan products. So bottom line, I use them. Do I use them all the time in every meal, no. But I use them in this cookbook. How often you make and eat things is your own damn business. But I stand behind the vegan food products at the grocery store because at the end of the day ain't nobody got time to make every single thing from scratch. I think cutting some obvious corners in the kitchen is necessary. I also get that not everyone has the same access to the products I do, so in most cases you can make substitutions for whatever you can't find. But you might be surprised at what you'll find at your local grocery stores if you've never looked before. I encourage you to find and buy things like nondairy milk, vegan butter, vegan mayonnaise, vegan cheese, vegan meat, and anything else that might help you avoid a ton of frustration. For example, *coconut whipped topping* is so damn good and consistent, whereas making your own can lead to less-than-perfect results. Buy these things, if you like them, because demand equals supply, and we've already managed to start collapsing the dairy industry with this monumental takeover so I support it ALL! Some people don't, but I assume if you follow what I do, you too are overjoyed at finding new things to try on the shelf! The choice is yours. Find and support the brands that you love—below are just a few of my favorites.

Vegan cheese is so good. If you've been scared to try it, it's better than it's ever been! Products come by the slice, brick, and already shredded for your convenience. If you can only find slices, you can just shred the whole stack of them on a box grater. Daiya has a line of shreds called the Cutting Board Collection that melts and tastes amazing, and I prefer these over the original formula that's still on the shelf. Violife also makes great shreds. For slices, I like Follow Your Heart/Earth Island, Field Roast Chao Slices, and Violife. Violife feta is to die for. And for cream cheese, I use Tofutti or Kite Hill plain almond milk cream cheese. I've had some pretty good products in Europe but I can't speak to their melting capabilities.

Vegan deli slices are what they sound like: meatless deli slices! I usually use the Tofurky brand slices myself.

Veggie ground round is a meatless ground *beef* substitute. There are plenty on the market, so find your fave and use it!

Soy curls are the best thing ever! Really the only kind that I've ever seen are a brand called Butler Soy Curls. You can order them online easily rather than running around to a ton of stores searching the shelves. But in all recipes calling for soy curls, you can sub with the same amount of *unbreaded vegan chicken* pieces. I personally like the slow-roasted pieces by Tofurky, or firm tofu shredded by hand could work as well.

Frozen french fries and tater tots are vegan, hallelujah!

Frozen vegan puff pastry is magic. The package you find may not be certified vegan and that's OK. It's likely accidentally vegan, so just double-check the ingredients. Puff pastry is made with vegetable shortening and/or vegetable oils, not often butter. But again, just check. And puff pastry is not phyllo, so do not swap them. And do not attempt to make your own puff pastry unless you want to have a breakdown on your kitchen floor.

stuff you need

As far as equipment goes, I'm not throwing anything new at you. If you have my first book, *Vegan Comfort Classics,* I outline the handy essentials I use all the time and the same goes for this book. You don't need a waffle iron, but I will emphasize the importance of investing in a good high-powered blender. That's the big game-changer if you want to level up your recipes. I've even adopted using Silpat mats instead of parchment paper…sometimes! Parchment still works best for getting certain foods crispy. I've specified in the recipes what will work best.

When it comes to ingredients, don't worry! You don't need to get ALL of this stuff before you dive into the cookbook. I find that building a pantry gradually is key, and there may be some things in this list that you straight up don't like or don't want to buy. That's fine, too! Find suitable substitutes that bring *YOU* joy, but I thought this list would be helpful when you're thinking about grocery shopping. It's also laid out the way a typical grocery store is!

FRUITS

Gala apples

Granny Smith apples

bananas

grapefruits

lemons

limes

frozen mango chunks

oranges

strawberries

VEGETABLES

arugula

avocados

bean sprouts

fresh or frozen beets

bok choy

broccoli

brussels sprouts

napa cabbage

purple cabbage

carrots

cauliflower

celery

fresh or frozen corn kernels

English cucumber

garlic

ginger

fresh or frozen green beans

jalapeños

curly kale

lacinato kale

green leaf lettuce

mesclun greens/spring mix

microgreens

romaine lettuce

cremini mushrooms

shiitake mushrooms

green onions

red onions

white or yellow onions

fresh or frozen peas

sugar snap peas

green bell peppers

red bell peppers

poblano peppers

shishito peppers

russet potatoes

white or yellow waxy potatoes

shallots

spinach

kabocha squash

sweet potatoes

Japanese sweet potatoes

cocktail/Campari tomatoes

grape tomatoes

hothouse tomatoes

sundried tomatoes

vine tomatoes

zucchini

FRESH HERBS

basil

chives

cilantro

dill

mint

oregano

parsley

rosemary

sage

tarragon

thyme

CANNED OR JARRED VEGETABLES & BEANS

marinated artichokes

black beans

butter beans

cannellini beans

chipotle peppers in adobo sauce

split mung beans

young green jackfruit in brine

brown lentils

kalamata olives

roasted red peppers

garlic dill pickles

pure pumpkin puree

fire-roasted tomatoes

sauerkraut

PREPARED CONDIMENTS

agave nectar

vegan beef bouillon base or cubes

buffalo-style hot sauce

vegan chicken bouillon base or cubes

vegetable broth powder

capers

green curry paste

red curry paste

gochujang

hummus

pickled jalapeños

raspberry jam

vegan-friendly kimchi

liquid smoke

maple syrup

marinara sauce

vegan mayonnaise

mellow white miso

Dijon mustard

prepared yellow mustard

peanut butter

vegan pesto

pizza sauce

red tomato salsa

salsa verde

Sriracha

tahini

gluten-free tamari

tomato paste

vegan Worcestershire

DRIED SPICES

basil

ground cardamom

cayenne pepper

chili flakes

chili powder

ground cinnamon

Chinese five spice

chipotle chili powder

citric acid

ground coriander

ground cumin

curry powder

dill seed

dill weed

dulse granules

garam masala

granulated garlic powder

ground ginger

kala namak

mustard seed

ground nutmeg

dehydrated minced onion

onion powder

oregano

smoked paprika

ground black pepper

ground white pepper

ground sage

fine-ground sea salt

Maldon sea salt flakes

thyme

ground turmeric

Old Bay Seasoning

OILS & VINEGARS

avocado oil

Chiu chow chili oil (garlic chili oil)

coconut oil

extra-virgin olive oil

light olive oil

toasted sesame oil

neutral vegetable oil

apple cider vinegar

balsamic vinegar

seasoned & unseasoned
rice vinegar

white distilled vinegar

white wine vinegar

BAKING STAPLES

baking powder

baking soda

bread crumbs (panko and Italian style)

cacao nibs

raw cacao powder

dairy-free baking chocolate

vegan chocolate chips

cocoa powder

canned coconut cream

canned full-fat coconut milk

flaked coconut

unsweetened shredded coconut

cornmeal

cornstarch

almond flour

all-purpose flour

gluten-free all-purpose flour

cake flour

chickpea/gram flour

whole wheat flour

nutritional yeast

gluten-free rolled oats

golden flax meal

brown sugar

organic granulated cane sugar

coconut sugar

confectioners' sugar

demerara sugar

tapioca flour

vanilla extract

NUTS, SEEDS & DRIED FRUIT

dried blueberries

raw cashews

roasted cashews

chia seeds

dried currants

Medjool dates

hemp hearts

salted peanuts

spicy peanuts

pecans

salted shelled pistachios

poppy seeds

pumpkin seeds

raisins

black/white sesame seeds

sunflower seeds

walnuts

GRAINS & PASTA

buckwheat

buckwheat soba

chow mein

farro

linguine

elbow macaroni

pappardelle

large pasta shells

organic popcorn kernels

quinoa

ramen

dried rice paper sheets

brown rice

rotini

spaghetti

udon

BREADS

Italian-style baguette

sesame seed buns

store-bought pizza dough

sourdough loaf

sprouted-grain sandwich bread

large flour tortillas

small corn tortillas

flat tostada shells

lavash wraps

SNACK FOODS

vegan cheese puffs

bagel chips

jalapeño-flavored kettle chips

ruffled potato chips

organic corn tortilla chips

dehydrated vegetable chips

Unreal Dark Chocolate
Crispy Gems

Fritos

mini pretzels

rice senbei snacks

sesame sticks

seaweed snacks

natural wasabi peas

VEGAN DAIRY

coconut whipped topping

vegan butter sticks

vegan cheese (shreds, slices,
Parmesan, feta, Cheddar)

nondairy milk (soy, almond,
cashew, oat, etc.)

vegan sour cream

vegan cream cheese

VEGAN MEATS

Butler Soy Curls

unbreaded vegan chicken pieces

vegan pepperoni

veggie ground round

vegan Italian sausages or
bratwurst-style sausages

tempeh

tofu

FROZEN CONVENIENCE FOODS

frozen french fries

frozen hash browns

frozen puff pastry

frozen tater tots

vegan wonton wrappers

BEVERAGES

club soda

dry white wine

breakfast stuff

This chapter has you covered, with stuff like buttery, flaky scones, or danishes stuffed with sausage and scramble. It's what you actually want to serve your friends for brunch, like breakfast pizza or totchos! And I couldn't forget some breakfast sweets like apple crumble muffins or crunchy coconut granola. And I even threw in some uber healthy choices like juices and my go-to smoothie. Start your day the vegan way and get inspired to swap out the predictable eggs and bacon for something more…plantiful.

TOFU SCRAMBLE

 10 mins. ⬛ 15 mins.

INGREDIENTS

¼	cup minced shallot (about 1 shallot)
1	tablespoon avocado oil, neutral vegetable oil, or vegan butter
1	brick (16 oz/450 g) medium-firm or firm tofu (about 3 cups crumbled)
2	teaspoons minced garlic (about 1 large clove)
2	tablespoons nutritional yeast
½	teaspoon ground turmeric
½	teaspoon smoked paprika
½–1	teaspoon sea salt
½	teaspoon ground black pepper
	Unsweetened nondairy milk

OPTIONAL MIX-INS

Use Veggies you have on hand that need to get eaten, such as spinach or kale, grape tomatoes, mushrooms

¼	cup finely chopped chives
½	teaspoon kala namak

MAKES ABOUT 3 CUPS If you're vegan or vegan-ish, of course you know how to make a tofu scramble. It's like the first thing that comes up when you search "what do vegans eat?" But I make a mean one, and I don't think there are enough clever, easy breakfast ideas utilizing the magic scram. I included this recipe because, like I said, I want you to treat my cookbooks like vegan bibles and this NEEDS to be part of the scripture. It's great on its own any day of the week, but on the following pages you'll see ways to make **Breakfast Za (page 20)**, **Breakfast Totchos (page 23)**, and **Stuffed Breakfast Danishes (page 24)** with it too. Use this as a guideline, but definitely jazz up your scram however you want. You're the one eating it, after all!

Tofu comes both in water-packed and vacuum-packed styles. Water-packed tends to have a lot more moisture and you'll need to squeeze out some of the excess moisture. In the case of vacuum-packed tofu, which is drier, you might want to reconstitute your tofu at the end with some nondairy milk to get more of a scrambled egg texture. Either way works—it's really entirely up to you and what texture you prefer.

In a cast-iron or nonstick pan over medium heat, sauté the shallot in oil or vegan butter for about 1 minute, until soft.

Using your hands, crumble the tofu into small chunks, like scrambled eggs, directly into the pan. Add the garlic and sauté for 2 to 3 minutes. Then stir in the nutritional yeast, turmeric, paprika, ½ teaspoon sea salt, and black pepper.

If you're bulking up your scram with veggies, add them in just after you mix in the seasonings. Continue frying for 3 to 4 more minutes. If you used a water-packed tofu, it's usually perfect at this point. If the mixture is too dry for your liking, add a little bit of nondairy milk, up to ¼ cup, until the desired consistency is achieved. If you add the nondairy milk, you'll likely need to cook the scramble for another 2 minutes or so.

Stir in the chives during the last 30 seconds. Remove the pan from the heat and stir in the kala namak. Add up to another ½ teaspoon of sea salt to your taste if necessary. Using kala namak often makes it salty enough, but if you don't use it, you will likely need to add more salt to taste.

Store in the fridge and consume within 3 days.

HOT TIP If you're going to make the **Mushroom Kimchi Omelet (page 18)**, **Breakfast Za (page 20)**, **Stuffed Breakfast Danishes (page 24)**, or **Breakfast Totchos (page 23)**, be sure you reserve some scramble without veggies mixed in—chives are OK!

HOT TIP Level up your scram and add warm **Egg Yolk Sauce (page 188)** on top for something a lil' extra!

MUNG BEAN SCRAMBLE

10 mins.   25 mins.

60 mins. soaking

INGREDIENTS

1	cup dried moong dal (split mung beans)
1	teaspoon sea salt, plus more to taste
1	tablespoon avocado oil, neutral vegetable oil, or vegan butter
¼	cup minced shallot (about 1 shallot)
2	teaspoons minced garlic (about 1 large clove)
2	tablespoons nutritional yeast
½	teaspoon ground turmeric
½	teaspoon smoked paprika
½	teaspoon ground black pepper
¼	cup canned coconut cream

OPTIONAL MIX-INS

Use veggies you have that need to get eaten!

¼	cup finely chopped chives
½	teaspoon kala namak

MAKES ABOUT 3 CUPS I wanted to make an alt version of a scramble and use something extra nutritious. Split mung beans are incredible beans often seen in Indian or Filipinx cooking. But my intro to them was from that very realistic egglike product that *just* came onto the market a couple years ago. Rather than trying to engineer an exact replica at home (which I did test, and I wasn't too impressed), I thought why don't I eat these beans whole? They're delicious and happen to look like scrambled eggs if I add all the same things from the tofu scram. So voilà! This is super inexpensive, as you'll be purchasing the dry beans and they only need a little soaking and some boiling. Adding coconut cream into the mix gives them some much-needed fat and a nice creamy texture.

Cover the beans with hot water in a large bowl and let them soak for 1 hour. Drain and then place beans in a large pot, cover with fresh water about 1 inch higher than the top of the beans, and add 1 teaspoon sea salt. Bring to a boil over high heat and cook for 20 minutes uncovered. Lower the heat if necessary to keep at a boil without boiling over, and stir occasionally. Once cooked, the beans should be slightly expanded. They should have a similar texture to canned lentils, slightly firm and not mushy. Drain any excess water after boiling, if necessary.

Heat a nonstick pan over medium heat with the oil or vegan butter and sauté the shallot and garlic for about 1 minute, until soft and fragrant. Add any chopped veggies you like just after cooking the shallot and garlic. Allow the veggies to mostly cook before adding the mung beans, as you don't want to overcook the beans or they will get quite mushy.

Add the cooked beans, nutritional yeast, turmeric, paprika, and black pepper and stir to combine. Cook another 3 minutes, stirring occasionally.

Stir in the coconut cream, allowing it to soften and melt on the bottom of the pan. Combine well and cook for about 1 more minute. Remove the pan from the heat and stir in the chives and kala namak or more sea salt to taste.

Store in the fridge and consume within 3 days.

HOT TIP Reserve Mung Bean Scramble without veggies mixed in if you're making **Breakfast Za (page 20), Stuffed Breakfast Danishes (page 24),** or **Savory Broken Scone Breakfast Muffins (page 32).**

MUSHROOM KIMCHI OMELET

 15 mins. 20–25 mins.

*use leftover Tofu Scramble
(page 14; optional)*

INGREDIENTS

1   cup leftover Tofu Scramble (no veggies mixed in) or 1 cup crumbled medium-firm or firm tofu

½   cup unsweetened nondairy milk, plus more as needed

3   tablespoons chickpea flour

2   tablespoons tapioca flour (can substitute cornstarch)

1   tablespoon nutritional yeast, plus more as needed

½   teaspoon garlic powder

½   teaspoon onion powder

½   teaspoon sea salt or kala namak

½   teaspoon ground black pepper

¼   teaspoon ground turmeric

2   tablespoons vegan butter, divided

1   cup sliced cremini mushrooms

¼   cup finely chopped red onion

⅓   cup store-bought vegan kimchi, divided

½   cup vegan mozzarella shreds, divided

1   tablespoon finely chopped green onion, for garnish

MAKES 2 LARGE OMELETS If you have some leftover Tofu Scramble, you can whip it into a batter for this scrumptious omelet! Of course, it can be made from scratch with plain tofu as well. Either way, you're going to love stuffing these babies with all kinds of things, but just make sure there's always some vegan cheese in the mix, as that's gonna help make it stick together, ya dig?

In a high-powered blender, combine the scramble or tofu, nondairy milk, chickpea flour, tapioca flour, nutritional yeast, garlic powder, onion powder, sea salt, black pepper, and turmeric until very smooth. You should have a slightly thick batter that you can scoop but that still can slide out of a cup or off a spoon easily. Add a bit more non-dairy milk, if necessary.

Heat a nonstick pan over medium heat. Add 1 tablespoon of the vegan butter, the mushrooms, and onion, and cook for 4 to 5 minutes, until mostly cooked and slightly caramelized. Transfer to a dish and set aside.

Place the pan back over medium-low heat. Take ½ tablespoon of the vegan butter and coat the surface of the pan. Pour ½ cup of the omelet batter into the center and use a spatula to spread the batter out into a circle 8 to 9 inches wide. It will take 3 to 4 minutes to cook on the first side.

You'll notice the batter cooking through and getting darker in color around the perimeter and parts of the middle of the omelet. At this point, add half the mushrooms and onion, half the kimchi, and half the cheese shreds to one side of the omelet. Place a lid on the pan and turn the heat to low. Continue cooking for 1 to 2 minutes. Then, using a spatula, lift the empty side of the omelet and fold it over the filled side to create a half-moon shape. Place the lid back on the pan and cook for 1 to 2 more minutes. If you can flip the omelet easily to cook the other side for another minute, you can, or turn the heat off and leave the lid on for another minute or so to cook it through. The omelet shouldn't have a bitter taste from undercooked chickpea flour if you've cooked it thoroughly. Transfer to a plate, garnish with green onion, and serve immediately.

Cook the second omelet the same way using the remaining ½ tablespoon butter to coat the pan before adding the rest of the omelet batter. You can also refrigerate the batter and fillings up to 3 days for another breakfast during the week.

BREAKFAST ZA

 20 mins. 25 mins.

use leftover Tofu Scramble (page 14) or Mung Bean Scramble (page 17)

leftover Egg Yolk Sauce (page 188)

Tempeh Bacon Chunks (page 100; optional)

INGREDIENTS

1	cup crumbled vegan sausage or Tempeh Bacon Chunks
1	tablespoon olive oil
	All-purpose flour, for dusting
1	store-bought pizza dough
½	cup salsa verde
2	cups vegan mozzarella shreds
½	cup finely chopped kale, stems removed
⅓	cup finely chopped green onion (white and green parts)
1	cup leftover Mung Bean Scramble or Tofu Scramble
¼	cup leftover Egg Yolk Sauce, warmed

MAKES 4 SERVINGS/4 LARGE SLICES Breakfast AND pizza! No, it's not a joke. Mixing breakfast stuff with dinner stuff or lunch stuff is what I live for! Remember my breakfast lasagna? This pie comes together quickly if you've got leftover scram and egg yolk sauce. Feel free to throw some homemade vegan bacon on here, too, but truthfully I live for adding vegan sausage to anything I can. A spicy one goes really nice here. And there's no need for laboring over dough either 'cause you can buy it already proofed at the grocery store. Check your deli counter and if you don't see it but they're serving hot 'n' ready slices behind that glass, then they have dough in the back and they'll probably sell it to ya! You can make some Egg Yolk Sauce while the pizza is baking if you're not using leftover sauce. Whisk in the kala namak and extra vegan butter just before serving. If you're using leftover sauce, reheating it is fine. The kala namak will have lost some of its essence, but it's still delicious!

Preheat the oven to 475°F.

Heat a nonstick pan over medium heat and brown the vegan sausage for 5 to 6 minutes, or according to package directions. If you're using tempeh bacon chunks, they should already be baked and you don't need to reheat them.

Use your hand to coat the bottom of a large baking sheet with the olive oil.

Roll and stretch the pizza dough onto a floured surface into a mostly rectangular shape. Transfer it to the oiled baking sheet and then stretch it as best you can to the edges of the pan, being careful not to tear the dough.

Spread the salsa verde on the dough in an even layer, leaving about ¼ inch from the edge bare. Top with a third of the cheese shreds. Add half the kale, half the green onion, half the mung bean or tofu scramble, and half the vegan sausage or tempeh bacon, then repeat with a third of the cheese and the remaining kale, onion, scramble, and sausage or bacon so you get an even spread of all the toppings across the pizza. Then add the remaining cheese shreds on top.

Bake for 20 minutes or until the edges are golden brown and slightly crispy. Drizzle warm egg yolk sauce on top before serving.

HOT TIP If you can't get enough of that **Egg Yolk Sauce (page 188)**, drizzle some leftover sauce onto these totchos or mix it into the scramble before piling it on top.

BREAKFAST TOTCHOS

 10 mins.   35 mins.

use leftover Tofu Scramble (page 14) or Mung Bean Scramble (page 17)

Cilantro Sour Cream (page 189) or Jalapeño Ranch (page 190)

INGREDIENTS

1	package (about 1 lb/453 g) frozen tater tots
1	cup vegan Cheddar shreds
1	cup leftover Tofu Scramble or Mung Bean Scramble
½	cup canned black beans, drained and rinsed
½	cup grape tomatoes, halved (about 12 tomatoes)
¼	cup thinly sliced jalapeño (about 1 large jalapeño)
2	tablespoons finely chopped green onion (white and light green parts)
1	batch Cilantro Sour Cream, Jalapeño Ranch, or store-bought vegan sour cream

MAKES 2 LARGE OR 4 SMALL SERVINGS What can I really say about this breakfast contribution except that it's another tasty way to shovel scramble in your face! If you know me, you know I love tots, perhaps even more than french fries or onion rings…but do I have to pick? Don't you love all your children equally?! I can't pick. These totcho toppings are mere suggestions but it's how I fix mine—you do whatever you want.

Preheat the oven to 425°F.

Spread out the tater tots on a baking sheet in an even layer and bake for 25 to 35 minutes, until golden brown and very crispy, or bake according to package directions (bake time may vary depending on the brand).

Gather the tots closer together on the baking sheet to assemble the totchos or transfer them to a square baking dish if you'd rather. Top the tots with half the cheese, then add the scramble, black beans, tomatoes, jalapeños, remaining cheese, and green onion.

Broil on high for 4 to 5 minutes or until the cheese is melted and golden brown on top.

Drizzle with cilantro sour cream or jalapeño ranch, or use a store-bought vegan sour cream for serving.

STUFFED BREAKFAST DANISHES

 25 mins. 25 mins.

use leftover Tofu Scramble (page 14) or Mung Bean Scramble (page 17)

leftover Egg Yolk Sauce (page 188)

Tempeh Bacon Chunks (page 100; optional)

EVERYTHING TOPPING

1	tablespoon poppy seeds
1	tablespoon sesame seeds
1	tablespoon raw or roasted sunflower seeds
1	tablespoon dehydrated minced onion
1½	teaspoons granulated garlic powder
½	teaspoon sea salt

DANISHES

1	teaspoon olive oil
1	cup crumbled vegan sausage or Tempeh Bacon Chunks
1½	cups leftover Tofu Scramble or Mung Bean Scramble
¾	cup vegan Cheddar shreds
½	cup leftover Egg Yolk Sauce
1	package (1 lb/500 g) frozen vegan puff pastry, thawed overnight in the fridge
2	tablespoons melted vegan butter

MAKES 8 DANISHES This is breakfast deliciousness, stuffed into frozen puff pastry (more on that later!) so that we can take it to-go, no plate required. Because if you're a real wild thing like me, you grab this pocket full of love and make a mess in your car while you're driving to that appointment or meeting. Totally worth it! The finished baked danishes kinda look like that monster's face in *Stranger Things*, but you're going to bite *its* face, not the other way around.

Preheat the oven to 450°F. Line a large baking sheet with a Silpat mat or parchment paper.

To make the everything topping, in a small bowl, combine the poppy seeds, sesame seeds, sunflower seeds, onion, garlic powder, and sea salt and set aside.

To make the danishes, heat a nonstick pan over medium heat with the olive oil and brown the vegan sausage crumbles for 5 to 6 minutes, or according to package directions. If you're using tempeh bacon chunks, they should already be baked and don't need to be reheated. Transfer to a bowl. Add the scramble, cheese shreds, and egg yolk sauce and mix together. Ensure this mixture is either cold or at room temperature when you assemble the danishes with the pastry.

To prepare the puff pastry, lightly flour a work surface. Either cut the one large sheet of pastry in half or work with one sheet at a time if your package came with two prerolled sheets. Chill the other half in the fridge until ready to use.

Roll the pastry out into an 8 by 8-inch square. Cut the dough in half in each direction, making 4 squares. Place the dough squares on the prepared baking sheet. Measure out a scant ¼ cup of the filling and add it to the center of each square. Use the back of a spoon to gently flatten the mixture to reach just before the edges of the square, but avoid spreading to the corners since you're folding the corners over the top. Fold each corner over into the center and gently press into the filling. Leave a small seam between each folded corner and in the center for the filling to peek through. Pinch the four corners a bit with your fingers to keep the dough

sealed. Repeat with the other dough half and remaining filling, spacing the danishes about 1 inch apart.

Brush the melted vegan butter on top of the pastry corners and generously sprinkle with the everything topping, pressing gently with your fingers to help it stick. If the pastry feels soft and has no chill to it anymore, place the entire baking sheet in the freezer for 15 minutes before baking.

Bake for 20 minutes or until golden brown and crispy.

These are best eaten on the same day they're baked. But you can also store leftovers in the fridge and warm for 10 to 12 minutes in a 400°F oven before eating. You can also freeze the baked danishes, once cooled, between layers of parchment. Bake from frozen on a baking sheet in a 400°F oven for 15 to 20 minutes or until warmed through and the dough is crispy again.

TWO POTATO RÖSTI

40 mins.   25 mins.

INGREDIENTS

2	large russet potatoes, well scrubbed
1	small sweet potato, well scrubbed
1	teaspoon sea salt
1	tablespoon finely chopped fresh dill, plus more for garnish
1	tablespoon finely chopped chives, plus more for garnish
1	teaspoon granulated garlic powder
½	teaspoon ground black pepper
¼	teaspoon cayenne pepper
4	tablespoons vegan butter, divided
½	cup store-bought vegan sour cream, for garnish

MAKES 4 SERVINGS This traditional Swiss dish is a plate of crispy potatoes bigger than your face—a great way to start your morning if you ask me! Of course, two potatoes are better than one, so adding sweet potato to the mix puts it over the top. You might see traditional rösti served with eggs mixed in or plopped on top. Obviously I didn't do that, 'cause, vegan, but if you're looking to round out your brekky with some solid protein, add a side of scram (page 14) and some of that oh-so-addictive **Egg Yolk Sauce (page 188)** on top, too.

Use a box grater or the fine shredder of a food processor to shred the russet potatoes and sweet potato with peels on. You should have 4½ to 5 cups of shredded potatoes.

Place the shredded potatoes into a large colander and use your hands to combine with the sea salt. Let sit for 30 minutes in the sink to sweat out moisture. Place handfuls of the mixture in a nut milk bag, bamboo steamer cloth, or double-layered cheesecloth to squeeze out all the excess moisture. Repeat this until it's much drier and add it to a mixing bowl. Add the dill, chives, garlic powder, black pepper, and cayenne and combine with your hands, breaking up the shreds.

Heat a large nonstick pan with 2 tablespoons of the butter over medium heat. Allow it to completely melt and start to sizzle, about 2 minutes. Then add the shredded potatoes in an even layer, filling the pan. Press the mixture lightly into the pan with the back of a spatula, but do not make it too compact.

Let the potatoes cook for 8 to 10 minutes, until you see very little steam escaping and the top looks waxier and drier. You should easily be able to take a spatula around the edge to lift it up gently and check the doneness on the edges.

Take a large plate and invert it on top of the pan to flip the rösti cooked-side-up. Add the 2 remaining tablespoons of butter to the pan, let it melt and slightly bubble, and then slide the rösti back into the pan to cook on the other side for another 8 to 10 minutes. Lower the heat if the pan starts to become too hot or is starting to smoke. To serve, slide it out onto the plate, top with sour cream, and garnish with more fresh dill and chives.

SCONES 4 WAYS

 15–20 mins.   25 mins.

20–30 mins. refrigeration

BASE SCONE DOUGH

6	tablespoons vegan butter, cold and cubed, or refined coconut oil
2	cups all-purpose flour, plus more for dusting
1	tablespoon baking powder
1	teaspoon granulated sugar (can sub light brown sugar)
½	teaspoon sea salt (¾ teaspoon if using coconut oil)
¾	cup cold nondairy milk

MAKES 8 SCONES Slightly crisp exterior and flaky buttery interior…no, I'm not describing myself. I'm talkin' scones and they're one of my fave things to bake. They're easy and you can add ALMOST whatever you want to the dough. You can use soy or nut milk for this recipe, though soy milk tends to get a higher rise. If you choose to use fruit as a mix-in (and I suggest you do!), the texture will be slightly different because there's so much more moisture. I found using dried blueberries to be the best way to go, but dried strawberries aren't very red or pretty so I still opted for fresh. Fresh or frozen fruit works, but if you can find dried or freeze-dried fruit, it'll give you the best outcome in the texture of your scones.

Preheat the oven to 450°F. Line a large baking sheet with a Silpat mat or parchment paper.

Place the vegan butter or coconut oil in the freezer for 10 to 15 minutes so it gets very cold.

In a large bowl, whisk together the flour, baking powder, sugar, and sea salt.

Continued

SCONES 4 WAYS

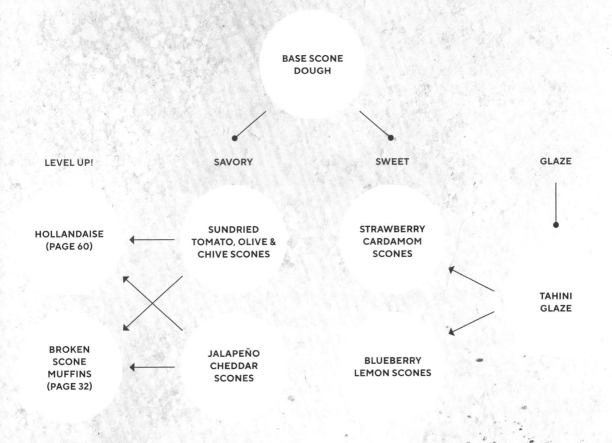

BASE SCONE
DOUGH

LEVEL UP!　　　　　　SAVORY　　　　　　　SWEET　　　　　　　GLAZE

HOLLANDAISE
(PAGE 60)

SUNDRIED
TOMATO, OLIVE &
CHIVE SCONES

STRAWBERRY
CARDAMOM
SCONES

TAHINI
GLAZE

BROKEN
SCONE
MUFFINS
(PAGE 32)

JALAPEÑO
CHEDDAR
SCONES

BLUEBERRY
LEMON SCONES

SCONES 4 WAYS

Continued

SUNDRIED TOMATO, OLIVE & CHIVE SCONES

¼	cup finely chopped sundried tomatoes (not packed in oil)
¼	cup finely chopped pitted kalamata olives
¼	cup finely chopped chives

JALAPEÑO CHEDDAR SCONES

1	cup vegan Cheddar shreds, divided
¾	cup finely chopped jalapeño, pith and seeds removed (about 2 large)

STRAWBERRY CARDAMOM SCONES

¾	cup finely chopped fresh strawberries (5 or 6 strawberries)
¼	cup packed light brown sugar
2	tablespoons orange zest (about 1 large orange)
2	teaspoons ground cinnamon
2	teaspoons ground cardamom

BLUEBERRY LEMON SCONES

1	cup dried blueberries
¼	cup packed light brown sugar
2	tablespoons lemon zest (2 or 3 lemons)
1	tablespoon lemon juice (about half a lemon)
1	tablespoon ground cinnamon

TOPPING
(ONLY FOR SWEET SCONES)

1	tablespoon nondairy milk
1½	tablespoons demerara sugar

Using a pastry blender (preferred) or a fork, cut the cold vegan butter or coconut oil into the dry ingredients so that small pea-size pieces are coated in flour throughout the mixture.

Add the ingredients for whatever variation of scones you're making and toss the mixture so the additions get coated in flour. For the jalapeño Cheddar, reserve about ¼ cup of cheese shreds to put on top of the scones.

Create a well in the middle of the mixture and pour the nondairy milk into it. If making the blueberry lemon scones, add the lemon juice to the nondairy milk beforehand. Use a spatula to fold the dough together until just combined; the dough should look ragged. Do not overmix.

Turn the ragged dough out onto a floured surface. Flour your hands and bring the dough together into a mound or ball. Gently flatten the top with your hand to form a circle and pack the sides of the dough in as well. The flat round should be 7 or 8 inches wide and at least 1 inch thick. The dough will stick together while you form the circle but will still have visible creases and cracks on the edges.

Lightly flour a dough cutter or sharp knife and cut the circle in half, and then in half the opposite direction to create quarters. Then cut each quarter in half to form 8 triangles. Lightly flour the dough cutter again and use it to lift each scone onto the prepared baking sheet, spaced apart by at least 1 inch. Top the jalapeño Cheddar scones with the remaining Cheddar shreds. If the dough does not feel chilled, refrigerate for 15 to 20 minutes before baking.

For sweet scones, brush with nondairy milk and sprinkle generously with demerara sugar just before baking.

Bake for 20 to 25 minutes, until the tops and edges are golden brown.

Remove the scones from the baking sheet and place on wire racks to cool. For best results, serve slightly warm. If desired, drizzle the sweet scones with the tahini glaze (on the facing page).

Store scones at room temperature for up to 4 days. Reheat leftovers by placing them in a 350°F oven for a few minutes until warmed through. You can freeze any leftover baked scones. If reheating from frozen, warm the scones in a 350°F oven for 12 to 15 minutes.

TAHINI GLAZE

10 mins.

MAKES ⅓ CUP (ENOUGH FOR 16 SCONES)

½   cup confectioners' sugar, sifted
2   tablespoons tahini
2   tablespoons nondairy milk
½   teaspoon vanilla extract or paste

Whisk the confectioners' sugar, tahini, nondairy milk, and vanilla together in a bowl until very smooth and pourable. Drizzle a small amount of glaze off the end of a spoon across each cooled scone. The glaze will remain slightly sticky. Extra glaze can be stored in a container at room temperature or in the fridge for weeks. Add a bit more liquid to loosen up, if needed, before using again.

SAVORY BROKEN SCONE BREAKFAST MUFFINS

 15 mins. 65 mins.

*use leftover
Savory Scones (page 28)*

*leftover Mung Bean Scramble
(page 17; optional)*

INGREDIENTS

4	leftover savory scones
¼	cup finely chopped chives, divided
⅔	cup leftover Mung Bean Scramble or chickpea flour
3	cups frozen shredded hash browns, divided
1¼	cups vegan Cheddar shreds, divided
1½	cups unsweetened nondairy milk
2	tablespoons vegan butter
1	tablespoon white wine vinegar
1	tablespoon nutritional yeast
1	teaspoon baking powder
1	teaspoon sea salt
1	teaspoon onion powder
½	teaspoon ground black pepper
½	teaspoon chili powder, divided

MAKES 12 MUFFINS Here's an easy way to use up some of your leftover savory scones—but honestly, who would have leftover scones?! What I mean is, here's a way to level up those savory scones you deliberately reserved for this recipe. Take the **Jalapeño Cheddar** or **Sundried Tomato, Olive & Chive Scones (page 30)**, break 'em, and bake 'em into these grab 'n' go muffins! These taste kinda like biscuits and gravy with hash browns and more Cheddar added in, tipping the comfort food scale over the top. Really, don't even try to compare these to anything, 'cause you ain't had nothing like them before!

Preheat the oven to 375°F.

Break the scones into bite-size pieces and divide evenly into a 12-cup muffin pan. Take half the chives and distribute among the muffin cups.

In a high-powered blender, combine the leftover scramble or chickpea flour, 1 cup of the hash browns, ¼ cup of the vegan Cheddar shreds, the nondairy milk, vegan butter, white wine vinegar, nutritional yeast (you can leave this out if using the leftover mung bean scramble), baking powder, sea salt, onion powder, black pepper, and ¼ teaspoon of the chili powder. Blend on high speed until very smooth.

Pour the batter over the broken scones, dividing evenly among the cups. They should be nearly full.

Mix the remaining hash browns and cheese together and divide among the muffins as a top layer. Sprinkle with the remaining chives and chili powder.

Cover the muffin pan with foil, ensuring it slightly tents on top so the cheese doesn't stick and come off. Bake for 30 minutes. Uncover and bake for an additional 20 to 30 minutes, until a toothpick comes out mostly clean from the center. Broil for 5 minutes to crisp on top, if needed.

BAKED PEANUT BUTTER
& JAM OAT BARS

15 mins.   25 mins.

INGREDIENTS

1	tablespoon golden flax meal
3	tablespoons water
2	cups gluten-free rolled oats (not quick cooking)
1	cup gluten-free all-purpose flour
1	cup coconut sugar
¼	cup tapioca flour (can substitute arrowroot flour)
1	tablespoon baking powder
1	teaspoon sea salt
1	cup natural crunchy or smooth peanut butter
¾	cup nondairy milk
1	tablespoon vanilla extract
¼	cup favorite jam

MAKES 16 BARS I don't want to knock oatmeal—it's filling and healthy—but I'm not the biggest fan of mushy porridge for breakfast. I make it 'cause it's quick, but with a little planning you can bake that oatmeal with peanut butter into a bar dolloped with your fave jam…now we're talking. These are just the right amount of soft and chewy and make another great grab 'n' go brekky.

Preheat the oven to 350°F.

Line an 8 by 8-inch baking pan with parchment paper by cutting two strips both 8 inches wide and crossing them in the pan to create clean edges. Trim the excess overhang, if needed.

Combine the flax meal and water and set aside to thicken, 5 to 10 minutes.

In a large mixing bowl, combine the rolled oats, all-purpose flour, coconut sugar, tapioca flour, baking powder, and sea salt.

In a large liquid measuring cup or another mixing bowl, combine the peanut butter, nondairy milk, and vanilla with the thickened flax meal mixture until smooth. Add this to the mixing bowl of dry ingredients and fold together until fully combined.

Spread the mixture evenly into the baking pan all the way to the edges. Take a dough cutter or knife and lightly score or mark every 2 inches across in each direction, creating the indented lines for 16 square bars. Do not cut through the pan of oat bars at this stage.

Dollop about ½ teaspoon of jam on top of each square and gently press it with the back of the teaspoon into the top of each bar.

Bake for 25 minutes, until the edges are golden brown and the bars look soft and raised. Cool in the baking pan on a wire rack for 20 minutes before lifting out by the parchment paper edges and placing onto the wire rack. Slice bars where you made the scores.

Cool completely before storing leftovers in the fridge. You can warm slightly in the microwave for 30 seconds before eating. Consume within 7 days.

HOT TIP If you don't require these to be gluten-free, then you can use rolled oats that aren't specifically labelled as such, and you can substitute 1¼ cups of all-purpose flour for the GF and tapioca flours.

APPLE CRUMBLE MUFFINS

20 mins. 20–22 mins.

TOPPING

½	cup rolled oats (not quick cooking)
¼	cup coconut sugar
2	tablespoons cold vegan butter
½	teaspoon ground cinnamon
¼	teaspoon ground nutmeg

MUFFIN BATTER

2¼	cups peeled, cored, and finely diced Granny Smith or Gala apple (about 2 apples)
1	tablespoon lemon juice
1	cup nondairy milk
1	tablespoon apple cider vinegar
1	tablespoon golden flax meal
1	teaspoon vanilla extract
2	cups whole wheat flour
¾	cup coconut sugar
1¼	teaspoons baking powder
1	teaspoon ground cinnamon
½	teaspoon ground ginger
½	teaspoon ground nutmeg
½	teaspoon baking soda
½	teaspoon sea salt

MAKES 12 MUFFINS I'm a big fan of muffins—if it were acceptable to eat them for every meal, I would. So if you're on the same page and want a sweet, comforting treat for breakfast or brunch, look no further than these apple crumble muffins. They're spiced just right, have tart chunks of apple throughout, and the buttery topping not only makes them look appetizing but ties all the coziness together.

Preheat the oven to 375°F.

Use oil or vegan butter to grease the cups of a muffin pan or line with paper liners.

To make the topping, in a small mixing bowl, combine the rolled oats, coconut sugar, butter, cinnamon, and nutmeg and pinch it together with your fingers to break up the butter and create a crumbly topping. Place the topping in the fridge while you prepare the muffins.

To make the batter, in another bowl, toss the apples with the lemon juice and set aside.

In a small mixing bowl or liquid measuring cup, combine the nondairy milk, apple cider vinegar, flax meal, and vanilla and set aside to thicken while you prepare the rest of the batter.

In a large mixing bowl, combine the flour, coconut sugar, baking powder, cinnamon, ginger, nutmeg, baking soda, and sea salt.

Create a well in the middle of the dry ingredients and pour in the milk mixture as well as the apples. Fold with a spatula until combined and no dry ingredients are visible, but do not overmix.

Portion a heaping ¼ cup of batter into each muffin cup. If there is any leftover batter, divide it among the cups; they should be quite full. Add about a tablespoon of the topping onto each muffin and gently press it onto the top so it sticks.

Bake for 20 to 22 minutes or until a toothpick comes out clean from the center. Transfer the muffin pan to a wire rack and allow the muffins to cool for 20 minutes before gently removing from the pan, using a knife or small spatula to nudge them out.

Store the muffins at room temperature or in the fridge in a container with the lid on loose; do not keep them airtight. Consume within 5 to 7 days.

HOT TIP You can easily substitute brown sugar for the coconut sugar, and if you want to use other fruits like peaches or berries instead of apples, use the same total cup amount listed.

HOT TIP Before you eat it all, be sure to reserve 1¾ cups of this to make the **Rocky Road Bars (page 205)**!

CRUNCHY COCONUT GRANOLA

10 mins.　35–40 mins.

INGREDIENTS

2	cups gluten-free rolled oats (not quick cooking)
2	cups large coconut flakes
½	cup pecans, coarsely chopped
¼	cup chia seeds
¼	cup golden flax meal
¼	cup coconut sugar
1	teaspoon ground cinnamon
1	teaspoon ground ginger
1	teaspoon sea salt
¼	teaspoon ground nutmeg
½	cup maple syrup
⅓	cup melted coconut oil

MAKES 6 CUPS Homemade granola is way less expensive and more satisfying than the store-bought stuff. It lasts awhile, unless you eat it like a maniac, and it's got simpler ingredients. I'm obsessed with this crunchy coconut granola; it's so good, it even makes an appearance in a dessert (see hot tip). I love this recipe because you can mix it up by hand right on the baking sheet. Very little mess and no dishes to clean up! You can use either refined or virgin coconut oil, but the coconutty flavor of the virgin variety works well here.

Preheat the oven to 325°F. Line a large baking sheet with a Silpat mat or parchment paper.

Directly to the sheet, add the oats, coconut flakes, pecans, chia seeds, flax meal, coconut sugar, cinnamon, ginger, sea salt, and nutmeg. Gently mix this together with your hands to combine.

Drizzle with the maple syrup and melted coconut oil. Mix thoroughly with your hands and spread into an even layer.

Bake for 25 minutes. Toss and continue to bake for 10 to 15 minutes more, until golden. Let the granola cool completely on the baking sheet on a wire rack, then break it up and store in a jar or container for 3 to 4 weeks in a cool, dry place.

MY BLENDER JUICE 3 WAYS

 10 mins.

REAL GREEN JUICE

2   celery stalks, cut into quarters
1   large Granny Smith apple,
    cut away from core
3   large kale leaves
2   cups packed spinach
½   lemon, peel cut off
    Large handful of fresh parsley
    Handful of mint leaves (optional)
1   cup fresh filtered water

SUNNY CITRUS JUICE

3   small navel oranges, peel cut off
1   large grapefruit, peel cut off
1   lemon, peel cut off
1   lime, peel cut off
½   cup ice cubes, to blend with after
    straining (optional)

IMMUNE WARRIOR JUICE

1   cup fresh or frozen beet chunks
    (about 1 beet)
2   carrots, cut into quarters
1   large Gala apple, cut away from core
½   lemon, peel cut off
⅓   cup fresh ginger chunks
1   piece of raw turmeric or 1 teaspoon
    ground turmeric powder
1   cup fresh filtered water

MAKES 2 TO 3 CUPS (2 GLASSES) Get ready to feel alive! I swear, doing this tilts the scale in my favor and balances out ALL the vegan junk-food habits I've acquired. Devotees of Lauren in Real Life (my other YouTube channel) have seen my baggy-eyed self in my "What I Ate in a Day" vlogs standing at the counter milking juice through a bag one too many times! No fancy juicers or infomercials here, y'all. Juice isn't an everyday event for me, but sometimes I get on these kicks where I do it a few days in a row, and it feels great. So when the craving strikes or I have a bunch of stuff in the crisper that needs using up, I throw it in the blender and strain away.

I try to drink all the juice, two servings, spread out over an hour. This is ideal, but if you just can't do it and have no one to share with, definitely halve the recipes or refrigerate what's left and consume within 24 hours. Give it a shake or stir it up before drinking.

Peels can be left on everything (just wash stuff!) except citrus fruits. And the seeds from citrus will just get pulverized or caught in the strain, so don't worry too much about fishing them out of the fruit. It's important to note that if you don't have a high-powered blender, this whole thing isn't going to work for ya!

The Sunny Citrus Juice comes out quite pulpy and there isn't a way to avoid this unless you use a juicer. Personally I like my citrus juice pulpy and don't mind this.

For the Immune Warrior, after a couple good washes you won't have pink hands. But you could also wear latex gloves. I use latex gloves when I cut jalapeño peppers, so they do come in handy!

For each juice, add the ingredients to a high-powered blender, such as a Vitamix. Blend with the smoothie setting or until very smooth and there are no visible pieces of fruits or vegetables. You might need to use the baton to push the mixture into the blade while blending to get it going.

Pour the mixture into a nylon nut milk bag over a large bowl or liquid measuring cup. Gently squeeze the mixture to strain the juice from the pulp, like you're milking the sack of juice. Strain until most of the juice is in the bowl and only pulp remains in the nut milk bag.

MY FAVE SMOOTHIE

 10 mins.

INGREDIENTS

1–2	shots espresso or ¼ cup leftover strong coffee
¾	cup nondairy milk
1	frozen banana
2	pitted Medjool dates
3	tablespoons hemp hearts
2	tablespoons natural almond or peanut butter
1	tablespoon raw cacao powder
½	cup ice cubes

MAKES 1 SERVING (ABOUT 2 CUPS) I used to make a lot of smoothies when I first went vegan. The early days of hotforfoodblog.com posts are smoothie heavy! But eventually I was sorta over it. I'm not really a smoothie person, but smoothies give the illusion of health and self-care so I fell for them at the start of my vegan journey. The only one I've kept in rotation is this one, which has coffee in it—duh! I'm the kind of person who makes a pot of coffee or a French press full of coffee, drinks one or two cups, and then keeps the leftovers until the next day specifically to make this smoothie. It's your coffee and breakfast in one, with nutritious, filling things like hemp hearts, dates, and banana.

Add the coffee, nondairy milk, banana, dates, hemp hearts, almond or peanut butter, cacao powder, and ice cubes to a high-powered blender and blend on high until very smooth. This is best consumed immediately.

lunch stuff

You can eat all sorts of delicious stuff for lunch! Soups, sandwiches, and salads are great places to start, or you can meal prep and then make hearty grain bowls. I'm going to help you create the perfect ones! In this chapter you'll also make things like tortilla soup and corn chowder and transform the leftovers into other stuff you can eat for lunch. I also like grilled cheese with my soup, so there are four versions of that to keep you busy. And sometimes lunch stuff can also be dinner stuff. The beauty is you get to decide!

TORTILLA SOUP

30 mins. · 50 mins.

INGREDIENTS

1	tablespoon vegan chicken-flavored bouillon base or 2 cubes
6	cups hot water (or vegetable stock, if not using bouillon base or cubes)
2	cans (20 oz/567 g each) young green jackfruit in brine, rinsed and drained
2	tablespoons + about ¼ cup neutral vegetable oil, divided
1	cup diced onion (about 1 onion)
1	cup diced green bell pepper (about 1 pepper)
¼	cup finely chopped jalapeño, seeds included (1 large jalapeño)
2	tablespoons minced garlic (3 or 4 large cloves)
¼	cup corn flour or cornmeal (see hot tips)
½	tablespoon coconut sugar
1	teaspoon chipotle chili powder
1	teaspoon sea salt, plus more for seasoning the tortilla strips
½	teaspoon ground cumin
½	teaspoon smoked paprika
½	teaspoon dried sage
¼	teaspoon ground black pepper
1	can (28 oz/794 g) fire-roasted crushed tomatoes (about 3 cups)
1	cup diced fresh tomatoes (2 or 3 small vine tomatoes)
1	can (15 oz/425 g) black beans, drained and rinsed (about 1½ cups)
1	cup frozen or fresh corn kernels
3	tablespoons gluten-free tamari or low-sodium soy sauce
6	(5- to 6-inch) soft corn tortillas, sliced into ¼-inch strips
2	tablespoons lime juice (1 large lime)
1	cup chopped fresh cilantro
2	avocados, diced

MAKES 4 TO 6 SERVINGS (10 TO 12 CUPS) It's my tortilla soup you already know and love, but this time with a bit more oomph! I made a version of this soup a while back for an episode of *RECIPE?!* on my YouTube channel, and since then, it's been made many many times by y'all with rave reviews. But the point of this cookbook was to take those half-baked ideas I made up on the spot and perfect the recipes so they're foolproof and profesh. So I didn't deviate too much, but I thought jackfruit would make a great swap for the chicken in this, and I like the idea of adding corn flour to the broth to thicken it a little more.

Dissolve the vegan chicken-flavored bouillon in the hot water and set aside.

In a fine-mesh sieve over the sink, squeeze the excess moisture from the jackfruit. Shred with your fingers onto a clean tea towel and pat dry of excess moisture. Remove any seed pods or tough pieces and add the rest to a large mixing bowl. You will have about 3½ cups of shredded jackfruit. If you have a small food processor you could also pulse the jackfruit a couple of times until shredded into pieces and pick out the seed pods or tough pieces by hand.

In a large stockpot or Dutch oven over medium heat, heat 2 table-spoons of the oil. Add the onion and bell pepper, and sauté, stirring occasionally, for 5 to 6 minutes, until soft and fragrant. Add the jalapeño, garlic, and jackfruit and sauté for 4 minutes, stirring only once or twice to get some of the jackfruit browned. Add the corn flour, coconut sugar, chili powder, sea salt, cumin, smoked paprika, sage, and black pepper and thoroughly mix to coat everything, creating some browning on the bottom. Cook, stirring occasionally, for 3 to 4 minutes. Add the fire-roasted and fresh tomatoes and stir to deglaze the pan for 1 minute. Add the black beans, corn, stock, and tamari or soy sauce. Stir to combine and turn the heat to medium-high. Bring to a simmer, stirring occasionally. Lower the heat to medium-low and cook for about 30 minutes.

While the soup simmers, heat a cast-iron skillet over medium-low with the remaining ¼ cup oil. Once the oil is hot, place one tortilla strip in the pan to make sure it bubbles. When it does, add a third of the tortilla strips and cook until golden brown and crispy, 3 to 4 minutes. Transfer to a paper towel–lined plate to absorb excess oil and sprinkle with the remaining sea salt. Repeat with

HOT TIPS If you only have cornmeal, pulse it in a spice grinder until it's fine and powdery like corn flour. Keep in mind that corn flour is finely ground cornmeal and is not cornstarch. Do not substitute cornstarch for this. The method is to thicken the soup slightly but also have a hint of corn flavor in the broth. You can also leave this out of the recipe and it will still be delicious.

Instead of jackfruit, you can also use 2 or 3 cups of smoked tofu or a vegan chicken product cut or pulled into shreds.

the remaining tortilla strips, adding a little more oil to the pan if needed. If any of the smaller strips begin to burn as you're frying, remove them as needed.

Just before serving, add the lime juice to the soup and mix well. Serve in bowls and garnish with the fried tortilla strips, cilantro, and avocado. Reserve 3 cups of the soup for **Red Sauce Enchiladas (page 48)** and 1 cup of the soup for **Chipotle Cheese Fries (page 51)**.

RED SAUCE ENCHILADAS

 25 mins.   45 mins.

use leftover Tortilla Soup
(page 46)

RED SAUCE
(MAKES ABOUT 4 CUPS)

3   cups leftover Tortilla Soup

¼   cup canned chipotle peppers
    in adobo sauce

2   tablespoons vegan Worcestershire

FILLING

1   large poblano pepper

1   tablespoon avocado oil or
    neutral vegetable oil

2½ cups diced zucchini (about 1 large)

1   cup diced red onion (about 1 onion)

2   teaspoons minced garlic
    (about 1 large clove)

½   cup frozen or fresh corn kernels

¼   cup finely chopped cilantro,
    plus more for garnish

½   teaspoon sea salt

½   teaspoon ground black pepper

ENCHILADAS

2   cups vegan mozzarella shreds

12 (5- to 6-inch) soft corn tortillas

MAKES 4 SERVINGS Sometimes it feels like a homemade soup will last for eons, especially if you're a household of one or two people. So ARE ya ready to level up more leftovers?! Freezing leftover soup is obvi a no-brainer, but you can use the Tortilla Soup to make these easy Red Sauce Enchiladas for another filling and spicy dinner idea. The red sauce is about a medium level of heat, so reduce or increase the amount of chipotle peppers in adobo sauce to your liking.

Preheat the oven to 375°F.

To make the sauce, add the leftover tortilla soup, chipotle peppers, and vegan Worcestershire to a high-powered blender. Blend until smooth and set aside.

To make the filling, first char the poblano. If using a stovetop, hold the pepper over an open flame using metal tongs, rotating slowly to blister and char for about 4 minutes, until juicy. If using an oven, roast under the broiler on a baking sheet for 6 to 8 minutes per side, turning every so often. Place the charred pepper in a plastic bag and seal it. This will allow it to sweat and steam so you can remove the skin easily. Peel the skin off, de-pith, de-seed, dice, and set aside.

In a large cast-iron or nonstick pan over medium heat, warm the oil. Add the zucchini, red onion, garlic, corn, cilantro, sea salt, and black pepper. Cook for 6 to 8 minutes, stirring occasionally, until the zucchini is soft and the water has evaporated. Turn off the heat, add the diced poblano pepper, and stir to combine.

In a large baking dish that's either 8 by 11 inches or 9 by 13 inches, spread 1 cup of the enchilada sauce in an even layer. To assemble the enchiladas, sprinkle about 1 tablespoon of the cheese shreds onto a tortilla and add a scant 2 tablespoons of filling. Roll the tortilla tight and place into the dish seam-side down. Repeat with the remaining tortillas, creating 2 rows of 6. Sprinkle any remaining filling on top. Pour the remaining sauce on top and sprinkle with the remaining cheese. Tightly cover with foil and bake for 20 to 25 minutes, until the cheese is melted. Uncover and broil for 5 minutes, until golden brown and crispy. Garnish with more fresh cilantro before serving.

HOT TIP You'll use one more whole chipotle pepper in adobo sauce for the **Chipotle Cheese Fries (page 51)**, or you can blend any leftover chipotle peppers and sauce from the can with vegan mayonnaise to make a chipotle aioli or freeze the remainder and thaw before using in other recipes.

CHIPOTLE CHEESE FRIES

 15 mins. 30–50 mins.

*use leftover Tortilla Soup
(page 46)*

*homemade potato wedges
from Fries & Salad (page 80)
or frozen french fries*

Homemade potato wedges from
Fries & Salad or frozen french fries,
baked according to instructions

CHIPOTLE CHEESE SAUCE
(MAKES 1¼ CUPS)

1	cup leftover Tortilla Soup
¾	cup cubed vegan medium or mature Cheddar cheese
1	whole canned chipotle pepper in adobo sauce

TOPPINGS

¼	cup crumbled vegan feta cheese (optional)
2	tablespoons finely chopped red onion
2	tablespoons finely chopped fresh cilantro

MAKES 2 SERVINGS Here's another way to level up the Tortilla Soup into a spicy chipotle cheese sauce that you'll keep coming back to! Homemade baked potato wedges are its ideal partner, but I also envision some kind of taco creation with this sauce drizzled on top, or you can straight up dunk tortilla chips in it. Or how about dipping some crispy taquitos into this! You could also use the sauce swirled into the **One Pot Mac n' Cheese (page 110)** if you're looking to kick up the heat there. This dish is a medium level of heat, so adjust the amount of chipotle peppers in adobo sauce if needed.

Have the baked fries ready on a lined baking sheet. Turn the oven to broil.

To make the cheese sauce, if your leftover soup is cold from the fridge, microwave it for 1 minute to heat it through. Add to a high-powered blender along with the vegan Cheddar and chipotle pepper until very smooth. (For the cheese, you can take a pack of cheese slices and cut into cubes or use a block—just try to find something pretty sharp and flavorful.)

Bring the baked fries together in a pile and pour the cheese sauce over the top. Place under the broiler for 5 minutes or until bubbling. Garnish with the vegan feta, red onion, and cilantro.

CREAMY GREEN PEA SOUP

 15 mins. 15 mins.

use Old Bay Croutons (page 197)

MAKES 4 SERVINGS (8 CUPS) This soup is going to make you love green peas, unless you're already a big fan like me! They're one of my fave veggies, and I always have frozen peas in my freezer. I throw them into quick pastas, salads, or any leftovers that need some green in 'em. And for bonus points: They're also a super source of protein! Traditionally, you probably think of split pea soup, but I tested that and I wasn't really into the muddy color for my aesthetic vision for this collection of recipes. The bright green pea was the winner for a creamy herby soup that's full of fresh flavor and can be made ultra quick!

INGREDIENTS

2	cups frozen or fresh peas
2	tablespoons olive oil
¾	cup finely chopped shallot (about 2 large)
2	tablespoons minced garlic (3 to 4 large cloves)
1	teaspoon fresh thyme leaves
2	teaspoons sea salt
1	teaspoon ground black pepper, plus more for garnish
4	cups low-sodium vegetable stock
1	can (13.5 oz/400 ml) full-fat coconut milk
1	tablespoon nutritional yeast
3	tablespoons finely chopped fresh dill, divided
3	tablespoons finely chopped fresh parsley, divided
2	tablespoons finely chopped fresh mint, divided
2	tablespoons lemon juice (about 1 lemon)
¼	cup plain vegan yogurt or sour cream
	Old Bay Croutons, for garnish (optional)

If using frozen peas, add them to a bowl and cover with water to defrost them. Drain and set aside.

In a large stockpot or Dutch oven over medium heat, heat the olive oil. Add the shallot and garlic and sauté for 3 minutes, until soft and fragrant. Add the thyme, sea salt, and black pepper and sauté for another 2 minutes. Transfer this mixture to a high-powered blender and add the peas, vegetable stock, coconut milk, nutritional yeast, 2 tablespoons of the dill, 2 tablespoons of the parsley, and 1 tablespoon of the mint, leaving the rest of the herbs for garnishing. Blend until very smooth. Pour back into the pot and set over medium heat. Just as it starts to bubble, turn the heat off and stir in the lemon juice.

Serve the soup with a swirl of plain yogurt or sour cream, top with croutons, and garnish with the remaining fresh herbs and ground black pepper, to taste.

CREAMY GREEN PEA SOUP WITH PASTA & PARMESAN

 5 mins. 10 mins.

use leftover Creamy Green Pea Soup (page 52)

MAKES 2 SERVINGS Here's a quick and delicious way to level up and devour more of the creamy green pea soup! I mean, adding pasta to anything makes it even better, plus the peppery arugula goes really well with all the fresh flavors.

INGREDIENTS

1	cup rotini pasta
½	cup fresh or frozen peas
3–4	cups leftover Creamy Green Pea Soup
1	cup arugula
¼	cup shredded vegan Parmesan
2	tablespoons finely chopped fresh basil
	Ground black pepper, to taste

Bring a pot of salted water to a boil and cook the pasta until al dente. In the last minute of cooking, add the peas. Drain the pasta and peas but do not rinse.

Heat up the leftover soup in the microwave or in a pot on the stove. Add the drained pasta and peas to it and then portion the soup to the serving bowls. If only consuming one serving, add the pasta and peas to the bowl and add the hot soup over top. Garnish with half of the arugula, vegan Parmesan shreds, and fresh basil, and serve with lots of black pepper.

Store the leftovers in separate containers so the pasta doesn't soak up the soup.

CORN CHOWDER

25 mins.   30 mins.

C 20 mins. soaking

INGREDIENTS

½	cup raw cashews
2½	cups frozen or fresh corn kernels
½	cup fresh water
1	cup finely chopped white or yellow onion (about 1 onion)
2	tablespoons avocado oil or neutral vegetable oil
1	cup finely chopped carrot (about 1 large carrot)
1	cup finely chopped celery (about 2 stalks)
2	tablespoons minced garlic (3 or 4 large cloves)
2	cups cubed white or yellow potato, ½-inch cubes (about 2 potatoes)
1	bay leaf
1	tablespoon fresh thyme (or 1 teaspoon dried)
½–1	teaspoon chili powder
½	teaspoon smoked paprika
1	teaspoon sea salt
1	teaspoon ground black pepper
4	cups low-sodium vegetable stock, divided
4	cups loose packed baby spinach, coarsely chopped
¼	cup finely chopped fresh dill, for garnish

MAKES 4 SERVINGS (ABOUT 7 CUPS) It's proven—y'all love my corn chowder! But the old recipe from the blog was always missing chunks of potatoes! Hello Lauren?! Look, I don't know everything and I'm always learning, so I thought it was worth putting this perfected corn chowder recipe in print. It's got a smooth, creamy base, lots of veg, and just the right amount of seasoning. Oh yeah, and lots of corn that you not only char and have floating in the mix but also blend into the broth to make this chowder extra corny. Make sure you reserve some leftovers so you can level them up into some pretty stellar ideas on the following pages! And if you really want, you can put the **Tempeh Bacon Chunks (page 100)** on top of your chowder to make it even heartier.

Soak the cashews in hot water for 20 minutes.

To char the corn, heat a large Dutch oven (which you can use to make the entire recipe) or a cast-iron pan over medium-high heat, add the frozen or fresh corn kernels, and cook for 8 to 10 minutes, tossing only once or twice to get char marks on the corn.

Drain and rinse the cashews from the soaking water and add to a high-powered blender with the fresh water and 1 cup of the charred corn kernels. Don't blend it yet; just set this aside.

In the Dutch oven or a large stockpot over medium heat, sauté the onion in the oil. Cook for 2 or 3 minutes, stirring occasionally with a wooden spoon, until soft. Add the carrot and celery to the pot and cook for 5 to 6 minutes, until soft and the moisture has been released.

Add the garlic, cubed potato, bay leaf, thyme, chili powder, smoked paprika, sea salt, and black pepper. Sauté for 1 or 2 more minutes. Add 2 cups of the vegetable stock and scrape the bottom of the pot to lift off any browned bits. Bring the soup to a simmer on medium-high heat. Cook for about 8 minutes, until the potatoes are just fork tender.

Remove 1 cup of the soup, being sure you don't get the bay leaf, and transfer it to the blender with the corn, water, and cashews. Blend on high until very smooth.

Add this blended mixture back into the pot along with the remaining charred corn and remaining vegetable stock and stir until

combined. Simmer on low for another 10 to 12 minutes, or until the potatoes are cooked through.

For serving, add the spinach to the bottom of each serving bowl and pour hot corn chowder on top. The spinach will wilt in a couple of minutes and then you can stir it around in the bowl to mix it up. This will keep the spinach bright and fresh. You're also doing this so you can use the leftover corn chowder to make **Corn Chowder Hollandaise (page 60)** and **Cacio e Pepe (page 58),** and you don't want to have spinach blended in the mix!

Garnish with the fresh dill, then serve. If reheating leftovers, you might need to add a bit of water or vegetable stock to get it creamy and smooth again.

CACIO E PEPE

 5 mins.   15 mins.

use leftover Corn Chowder
(page 56)

MAKES 2 OR 3 SERVINGS If you want to transform the Corn Chowder into a sauce for some noods, you've turned to the right page! Cacio e pepe is a pasta dish simply meaning "cheese and pepper." But I'm me, so I'm adding blended Corn Chowder in here for an extra level of depth and complexity. Trust me, whenever I blend stuff into other stuff, it works, and in this case it makes a perfectly silky sauce for this easy twist on cacio e pepe.

INGREDIENTS

½   package (1 lb/454 g) spaghetti

1½ cups leftover Corn Chowder

1   cup shredded vegan Parmesan, divided

1   teaspoon ground black pepper, plus more for garnish

2   tablespoons finely chopped fresh basil or parsley (optional)

Bring a large pot of salted water to a boil and cook the spaghetti until al dente. Reserve ¼ cup of the pasta water before draining. Do not rinse the pasta. Add the pasta back into the pot and set aside.

In a high-powered blender, add the leftover corn chowder, half of the vegan Parmesan, the black pepper, and the reserved pasta water. Blend until very smooth.

Add the blended sauce and the basil or parsley into the pot with the pasta. Heat over low, tossing to coat the pasta until heated through. Serve with remaining vegan Parmesan on top and extra black pepper.

If reheating leftovers, you'll need to add a bit of water or vegetable stock to get it creamy and smooth again, but truthfully this is best eaten the first time you make it. I wouldn't recommend it as another leftover.

CORN CHOWDER HOLLANDAISE

 5 mins. 2–3 mins.

use leftover Corn Chowder (page 56)

MAKES 1¼ CUPS Oh yes, the leftover Corn Chowder also works as a base to make a creamy tangy hollandaise sauce! Serve this alongside warm **Savory Scones (page 28)** or any other brunch or breakfast item you please.

INGREDIENTS

1	cup leftover Corn Chowder
¼	cup melted vegan butter
1	tablespoon nutritional yeast
1	tablespoon lemon juice
½	teaspoon sea salt
¼	teaspoon kala namak (optional)
⅛	teaspoon ground turmeric

If you're using leftover corn chowder that's cold, microwave it in a bowl with the butter to melt the butter and heat the chowder.

Add this to a high-powered blender with the nutritional yeast, lemon juice, sea salt, kala namak, and turmeric. Blend until very smooth.

If reheating after the hollandaise has been refrigerated, you'll need to add a little water or unsweetened nondairy milk to thin it out, as it will thicken up.

ZUPPA TOSCANA

⬦ 25 mins.   ﹋ 45 mins.

INGREDIENTS

2	tablespoons vegan chicken-flavored bouillon base or 4 cubes
5	cups hot water (or vegetable stock, if not using bouillon base or cubes)
1	tablespoon olive oil
4	vegan sausages, crumbled (spicy flavor preferred)
2	cups diced zucchini (about 1 large)
1	cup finely chopped yellow onion (about 1 onion)
½	cup finely chopped celery (about 1 stalk)
½	cup finely chopped carrot (about 1 carrot)
2	tablespoons minced garlic (3 or 4 large cloves)
2	teaspoons dried oregano
½	teaspoon smoked paprika
½	teaspoon chili flakes
4½	cups cubed yellow potato, ½-inch cubes (4 or 5 potatoes)
1	can (15 oz/425 g) cannellini beans, drained and rinsed (about 1½ cups)
1	can (13.5 oz/400 ml) full-fat coconut milk
3	cups stemmed and coarsely chopped curly kale
1	cup coarsely chopped fresh parsley
	Sea salt, to taste
1	teaspoon ground black pepper

MAKES 6 SERVINGS I'm hopping all over Italy in this book! From Rome, which is where **Cacio e Pepe (page 58)** originates, to Tuscany, with this hearty zuppa toscana. You mean it doesn't originate from Olive Garden, Lauren?! I mean, it does in all of our collective memory banks but not historically. You really don't need unlimited salad and breadsticks with this one, guys. This soup has so much packed into it that I think it's a fantastic nostalgic all-in-one meal. The spicy vegan sausage is key in this soup but you can also use the **Tempeh Bacon Chunks (page 100)** if you prefer something homemade, and I've included the instructions for that option as well.

Dissolve the vegan chicken-flavored bouillon or cubes in the hot water and set aside.

In a Dutch oven or stockpot over medium-high heat, add the olive oil and crumbled sausage. Brown for 5 to 6 minutes on one side and toss occasionally for another 4 to 5 minutes, until the sausage is browned and cooked through. Lower the heat as necessary to prevent burning. Cook time may vary depending on the brand of sausages you're using. (You can also use the tempeh bacon chunks and cook them the same way, once marinated, rather than baking them like in the original recipe.) Transfer the sausage to a bowl and set aside. Leave any residual brown pieces on the bottom of the pot for flavor!

To the pot, add the zucchini, onion, celery, carrot, garlic, oregano, smoked paprika, and chili flakes and sauté for 6 to 7 minutes, stirring occasionally, until softened, cooked, and reduced to about half the amount in size.

Add the potato and cook, stirring, for 2 minutes. Add the stock and increase to high heat to bring to a simmer, cooking the potato until just fork tender, about 8 minutes.

To a high-powered blender, add ⅓ cup of the cannellini beans, all the coconut milk, and 1 cup of the soup including the vegetables. Blend on high until very smooth. Add this back into the stockpot with the remaining cannellini beans. Cook over a low simmer for about 15 minutes. In the last minute, stir in the kale and parsley.

Taste the soup before serving and add up to 1 teaspoon of sea salt or to your taste, as well as the black pepper and the vegan sausage.

You can also add sausage separately to each serving to prevent it from getting too soggy.

If reheating leftovers, you may need to add some water or stock to thin out the soup slightly. This soup, like all of the soup recipes in this book, once cooled completely can be jarred and frozen. Thaw in the fridge and then reheat.

stuff to eat...for casual get-togethers

Having people over to eat should come with zero pressure. You should spend time enjoying yourself rather than worrying about whether every little detail is perfect. These ideas are simple to put together for small groups of friends and family, and much of the cooking and prep can be done in advance.

A BRUNCH AFFAIR

stuffed breakfast danishes
(page 24)

charred corn salad (page 150) with
crispy tofu fingers (page 92)

passion fruit slice (page 225)

mimosas + coffee…obvs!

Make the stuffed danishes a day in advance and freeze them. Heat them in
the oven as guests arrive. The passion fruit slice can also be made the day
before. You can prechar your corn for the salad and make the dressing, then
leave it in the fridge, and assemble your salad (dressing on the side) in the
morning before everyone arrives. Create a make-your-own-mimosa and
coffee bar somewhere away from the kitchen and give one of your guests
the task of making sure the coffee is always brewin'!

WEEKEND LUNCH HANGS

clubhouse sandwiches (page 66)
with french fries

chocolate chip corn cookies
(page 206) or snickledoodles
(page 209) or both!

kombucha…please!

Make the tofu and beet bacon for the sandwiches and bake the cookies the day before. Then reheat the sandwich stuff just before making and
serving them.

HOSTING A SMALL DINNER
(I NEVER DO MORE THAN 6 GUESTS!)

grilled romaine hearts (page 88)
served as a Caesar salad with old
bay croutons (page 197)

easy brussels sprouts pasta
(page 124)

mini strawberry tarts (page 233)
or galette with in-season fruit
(page 234)

lotsa wine…thanks!

Make your strawberry tarts or galette in the morning along with the croutons
and tahini Caesar dressing. The romaine hearts and pasta won't take long to
cook and put together while guests are having some wine and catching up.

CLUBHOUSE SANDWICH

🔪 15 mins. ♨ 40 mins.

BEET BACON

1 tablespoon gluten-free tamari or low-sodium soy sauce

½ tablespoon nutritional yeast

½ tablespoon neutral vegetable oil

½ tablespoon maple syrup

¾ teaspoon liquid smoke

¼ teaspoon smoked paprika

1 small red beet, sliced ¹⁄₁₆ to ⅛ inch thin with mandoline

SANDWICH

1 brick (16 oz/454 g) firm tofu

2 teaspoons vegan chicken-flavored bouillon or 1 cube

2 tablespoons water

3 tablespoons neutral vegetable oil, for frying

Sea salt and ground black pepper, to taste

9 slices white or whole wheat sandwich bread

⅔ cup vegan mayonnaise

4–6 pieces green leaf lettuce

1 large hothouse tomato, sliced thin

MAKES 3 SANDWICHES This clubhouse is classic, but with a twist! I swapped chicken and bacon for tofu and beets and it's over-the-top delicious. There was a time in my young adult years when if I saw a clubhouse on a menu, I got it. Nothing else mattered. I think you'll feel some emotions flooding in after one big ol' bite outta this sammie. The beet bacon really only works in sandwiches like this, so I don't recommend repurposing it in salads or pasta dishes.

Preheat the oven to 400°F. Line a baking sheet with a Silpat mat or parchment paper.

To make the beet bacon, mix together the tamari or soy sauce, nutritional yeast, oil, maple syrup, liquid smoke, and smoked paprika in a large bowl. Toss the beet slices in the marinade, coating both sides, and let them sit for about 10 minutes.

To make the sandwich, slice the tofu into slabs or squares from the largest side, ⅛ to ¼ inch thick. The slabs may vary slightly, but that's OK. You should have 9 or 10. Lay them out on another baking sheet. In a bowl, mix together the bouillon and water until combined. Brush this on both sides of the tofu slices and set them aside until the beet bacon is in the oven.

Lay each marinated beet slice on the prepared baking sheet slightly spaced apart. Bake for 10 to 15 minutes on the middle rack. You might need to remove any slices that have already crisped up and bake the remaining pieces another 5 to 10 minutes. These will burn very quickly, so check them every 2 minutes to make sure the beet bacon doesn't completely char on the edges or burn. The slices will have wrinkled edges and still feel a little soft but they will get slightly more crisp as they cool.

To fry the tofu, heat a cast-iron pan over medium heat with 1 tablespoon of the oil, coating the pan evenly. Add a sprinkle of sea salt and black pepper to the tops of the tofu slices and place that seasoned side down into the hot pan. Fry the tofu in batches. Fry on the first side 4 to 5 minutes. Sprinkle with more sea salt and black pepper and flip. Fry the other side for 3 to 4 minutes. Repeat, adding more oil to the pan before frying the next batch, until all the tofu is fried.

Lightly toast the bread and spread the vegan mayonnaise on the bottom slice. Top with the lettuce and tomato and overlap 2 tofu slices to fit on the bread. Then spread the vegan mayonnaise on

both sides of the middle piece of bread and place it on top of the tofu. Top with the lettuce, tomato, 1 slice of tofu, and about 6 pieces of beet bacon. Spread the vegan mayonnaise on the top slice and place it on top. Insert toothpicks into the center of the sandwich, forming a diamond. Slice diagonally between the toothpicks into 4 triangles. Repeat for the remaining sandwiches or store the extra tofu and beet bacon up to 5 days to make sandwiches from leftovers.

The tofu is still delicious on the sandwich if made ahead or eating leftovers. If you want it to be slightly warm on your sandwich, microwave the tofu slices for 30 seconds.

SPICY LENTIL WRAP

 15 mins.   8 mins.

*use Tahini Caesar Dressing
(page 200)*

INGREDIENTS

1	tablespoon olive oil
½	cup finely chopped yellow onion (about half an onion)
½	cup finely chopped red bell pepper (about half a pepper)
¼	cup finely chopped green onion, white and light green parts (about 2 onions)
2	teaspoons minced garlic (about 1 large clove)
¾	teaspoon sea salt, plus more to taste
½	teaspoon ground cumin
½	teaspoon ground black pepper
½	teaspoon chili flakes
1	can (15 oz/425 g) brown lentils (about 1¾ cups)
½	cup finely chopped parsley
1	tablespoon lemon juice (half a lemon)
2	tablespoons hot sauce
1	batch Tahini Caesar Dressing
4	lavash wraps
2	cups finely shredded green or napa cabbage

MAKES 4 WRAPS I wish I knew who this was, but one of you slid into my DMs requesting a version of Trader Joe's spicy lentil wrap. I had never tried this thing, but when I finally did, I was hooked! I'm usually not a fan of premade wraps sitting in the fridge at a grocery store. Often they're soggy and bland, but that one passed my test. Still, I wanted to create my own version, especially since most people don't have access to the store-bought one, and I wanted everyone to enjoy this simple, healthy wrap. It's not an exact copycat 'cause I didn't go with a harissa spread, but my Tahini Caesar Dressing with a little hot sauce does the trick. All I can say is, these are yummy!

In a nonstick skillet or cast-iron pan over medium heat, heat the olive oil. Sauté the onion, bell pepper, green onion, and garlic for 2 to 3 minutes. Add the sea salt, cumin, black pepper, and chili flakes and cook for another 2 minutes, until everything is softened and fragrant. Add the lentils, parsley, and lemon juice and cook for 2 to 3 minutes. Remove the pan from the heat and add more salt to taste, if needed.

You could let this mixture cool and then store it for preparing wraps during the week. If using leftover lentil filling from the fridge, I like to microwave it for 30 seconds to 1 minute before assembling the wrap.

To make the wrap, add the hot sauce to the Caesar dressing and combine well. Spread 2 tablespoons of the dressing on the first two-thirds of the lavash, leaving a third without any sauce. Spread ½ cup of cabbage across where the dressing is and add ½ cup of the lentil mixture spread out on top. Drizzle with 1 to 2 more tablespoons of dressing, then roll up tightly from the end with all the filling, and cut the roll in half.

FRIED ARTICHOKE SANDWICH

15 mins.　20 mins.

use Jalapeño Ranch (page 190)

MAKES 4 SANDWICHES Traveling and finding new vegan eats is what I love, and one of my stand-out meals is from The Arbor in Vancouver. They have lots of scrumptious menu items, but the best one is the southern fried artichoke sandwich. If you're ever out there, give it a try. This is more of an ode to that amazing sandwich and not a rip-off. The battered and fried artichokes have a satisfying crunch and a kind of buttery and tangy bite to them that you're going to love. And yes, it's messy to eat, which is the best part!

CABBAGE SLAW

2½   cups finely shredded purple cabbage
1   batch Jalapeño Ranch, divided
½   tablespoon lime juice (about half a lime)

FRIED ARTICHOKES

2–3   cups neutral vegetable oil, for frying
10–12 canned or jarred whole artichoke hearts (20 to 24 artichoke halves)
1¼   cups gluten-free all-purpose flour, divided
¾   cup cornstarch
1   teaspoon sea salt
1   teaspoon ground black pepper
½   teaspoon smoked paprika
½   teaspoon garlic powder
¼   teaspoon cayenne pepper
1–1½ cups club soda

SANDWICHES

4   sesame seed buns
1   dill pickle, sliced into thin rounds (about ¼ cup)

To make the cabbage slaw, combine the purple cabbage with 1 tablespoon of the jalapeño ranch and all the lime juice in a mixing bowl. Set aside in the fridge while you prepare the fried artichokes.

To make the fried artichokes, in a deep fryer or in a large heavy-bottom pot with a thermometer attached heat the fryer oil to 360°F. If using a pot, it should be around a third full of oil. Set aside a large baking sheet with a wire rack on top to place the fried artichokes on. Do not rest them on paper towels as they will become soggy.

Drain the artichoke hearts from the can or jar and cut them in half if they're whole. Gently squeeze out any excess water from the artichoke pieces by patting between paper towels or with a clean tea towel so that the artichokes aren't super wet.

To a large mixing bowl, add ½ cup of the gluten-free flour. In another large mixing bowl, whisk together the remaining ¾ cup of the flour, the cornstarch, sea salt, black pepper, smoked paprika, garlic powder, and cayenne.

Once the oil is to temperature, add 1 cup of the club soda to the flour mixture to start and gently whisk until combined. Add more club soda as needed to ensure the batter is loose enough to dip and dredge the artichokes but thick enough that it sticks and doesn't run right off too much. (The amount of liquid varies, as I find gluten-free flours to have varying hydration levels.) Use one hand to coat 4 or 5 artichoke halves in the flour dredge and then coat one piece at a time in the liquid batter. Lift each piece from the batter and let the excess drip off. Quickly place the battered

HOT TIP If you only make 1 or 2 sandwiches, you can use the remaining fried artichokes to make the **Dill Pickle Popcorn Snack Mix (page 181)**. Let the fried artichokes cool completely, freeze them on a baking sheet in a single layer, then put them in a freezer-safe bag or container. To cook the artichokes from frozen, preheat your oven to 400°F. Bake for 12 to 15 minutes, flipping halfway, until cooked through and crispy.

artichokes directly in the hot oil and fry the first batch for 4 to 6 minutes, until crispy and golden brown.

Use a slotted spoon or a pair of tongs to place the artichokes onto the wire rack, and continue frying in batches.

To make the sandwiches, lightly toast the buns. Spread the remaining jalapeño ranch on the inside of the top and bottom buns. Add the purple cabbage slaw to the bottom bun and top with pickles, 4 or 5 fried artichoke pieces, and the top bun.

stuff I eat…IRL

If you want a real look at what a cookbook author eats in a day, this is it. Nothing fancy, nothing complicated, but still damn delicious. This is a typical menu of food in my everyday life and it could even be used as a great starting point for those of you who want to give this vegan life a try and are struggling to make the switch! Remember, you don't have to go entirely vegan overnight. Start somewhere, anywhere, and if you still can't bear the taste of these (amazing) vegan cheese products, well, eliminating meat in even one or two meals a day or going vegan one day every week is still a monumental stepping-stone in a compassionate direction.

BREAKFAST

tofu scramble (page 14) with added veggies

toast with vegan butter (maybe some avocado, too!)

my blender juice (page 41)

coffee with vegan creamer (always!)

LUNCH

my everyday sandwich (page 75)   + reheated leftover soup

SNACK

classic onion dip (page 163)   + celery and carrot sticks

DINNER

bacon kale pasta (page 127)

MY EVERYDAY SANDWICH

 10 mins.

INGREDIENTS

2	slices sprouted-grain bread
1	tablespoon vegan mayonnaise
1	tablespoon Dijon mustard
1	leaf romaine lettuce, torn
2	tablespoons sauerkraut
4	slices vegan deli meat
2	slices vegan mature or medium Cheddar cheese
1	garlic dill pickle, thinly sliced lengthwise
	Ground black pepper, to taste

MAKES 1 SANDWICH I'm not going to tell ya how to make your go-to sandwich, but here is a little inspo to get ya started! It's also an easy transitional idea if you're not currently vegan. Swap that ham, turkey, pastrami, or salami (aka processed deli meats) for this equally satisfying and noncarcinogenic sandwich. (Sorry, just the cold hard truth!) But customize it however you want. You dig sloppy tomatoes on your sandwich, be my guest. You want to grill it a little? I'm cool with that. But this is the sandwich that fuels my days and nights while I'm working away on hot for food recipes. Sometimes I even eat it before noon, 'cause I can't think of anything else I'd rather eat when I'm starving!

Lightly toast the bread.

Spread the vegan mayonnaise on one slice of the toasted bread and Dijon on the other.

On the mayonnaise side, layer the romaine lettuce, sauerkraut, deli slices, vegan cheese, pickles, and black pepper to taste. Top with the other slice of bread with the Dijon facing down and slice diagonally. Enjoy!

HOT TIP Spice up your everyday sandwich with leftover sauces like **Jalapeño Ranch (page 190)** or **Tahini Caesar Dressing (page 200)** in replace of plain ol' mayo!

MY EVERYDAY ROASTED VEGETABLE SALAD

 20 mins.   25 mins.

use Use Up the Hummus Dressing (page 201) or any dressing of your choice

ROASTED VEGETABLES (TO FILL 1 LARGE BAKING SHEET)

3	cups halved brussels sprouts, outer layer and stem trimmed (about 18 brussels sprouts)
3	cups medium cauliflower florets, trimmed (about half a head)
3	cups cubed Japanese sweet potato (about 1 large potato)
1	cup large diced red onion (about half an onion)
3	tablespoons olive oil
1	teaspoon sea salt
1	teaspoon ground black pepper
½	teaspoon chili powder
½	teaspoon dried thyme (can use 1 teaspoon fresh if you have)

SALAD

	Pinch sea salt
4	cups packed curly kale, stemmed and finely chopped into ribbons
1	cup shredded or finely chopped purple cabbage
¼	cup dried currants
¼	cup toasted pumpkin seeds
¼	cup hemp hearts
1	batch Use Up the Hummus Dressing or any dressing of your choice
	Ground black pepper, to taste

MAKES 4 SERVINGS When there's been too many vegan doughnuts and chicken fingers in my meal plan, I turn to this salad. Old faithful, totally comforting, healthy, and filling. Listed below are the vegetables I typically roast, but you can work with whatever vegetables you have. But since I'm suggesting taking some of this leftover roasted veg and pulverizing it to make some **Roasted Vegetable Potstickers (page 78)**, I suggest always having a couple of cruciferous veg and some kind of potato. Some other stuff that'll work well are bell peppers, zucchini, squash, leeks, celery, carrot, cabbage, and broccoli. You want to fill a large baking sheet with cut-up vegetables, but don't overcrowd or they won't roast up as nicely!

Preheat the oven to 450°F.

To a large baking sheet, add the brussels sprouts, cauliflower, sweet potato, and red onion. For roasting vegetables, I don't line the baking sheet. They will get better color without Silpat or parchment, but it's personal preference!

Use your hands to coat the vegetables with the olive oil, sea salt, black pepper, chili powder, and thyme. Spread the vegetables out in an even layer.

Bake for 20 to 25 minutes, flipping halfway through baking, until the vegetables are tender and golden brown.

Meanwhile, sprinkle a pinch of salt on the kale and massage it until it wilts slightly and looks juicier. You can do this even if you're prepping the salad components in advance; just don't add dressing if you're storing it for a few days.

Top the kale with the cabbage, warm roasted vegetables, currants, pumpkin seeds, hemp hearts, and your dressing. Toss until well combined, and garnish with ground black pepper, for serving.

HOT TIP Reserve 2 cups of the mixed roasted vegetables to make the **Roasted Vegetable Potstickers (page 78).**

ROASTED VEGETABLE POTSTICKERS

 45 mins.   8 mins. per batch (24 mins. total)

use leftover roasted vegetables from My Everyday Roasted Vegetable Salad (page 76)

Sesame Soy Vinaigrette (page 201)

INGREDIENTS

5	shiitake mushrooms
2	cups leftover roasted vegetables
⅓	cup finely chopped or shredded napa cabbage
¼	cup finely chopped chives or green onion, plus more for garnish
2	teaspoons peeled and grated fresh ginger
2	tablespoons gluten-free tamari or low-sodium sauce
26	round vegan wonton wrappers
¼	cup sesame seeds
	Neutral vegetable oil, for pan-frying
1	batch Sesame Soy Vinaigrette, for serving

HOT TIP I like to peel a lot of fresh ginger, cut the big pieces into 1-inch knobs, and freeze them in a container. Then it's easier to grate fresh ginger on a microplane or throw a chunk into the blender if needed for a sauce. No need to thaw them before using.

MAKES 24 TO 26 POTSTICKERS This is a clever way to eat more vegetables and use up some you may have prepped for the week. I imagine by day two you're kinda over salad, or maybe that's just me! I whirled up two cups of leftover roasted veg and threw in some shiitakes, cabbage, chives, and ginger, and it made a surprisingly tasty potsticker. The sesame soy vinaigrette also makes the perfect accompaniment for these delicious morsels. The only challenge might be getting the hang of pleating your potstickers to look like the real deal… I suggest you hop on YouTube and get watching some tutorials (like I did!).

In a small food processor, pulse the shiitakes into a fine mince. Add the roasted vegetables and pulse until the mixture is about the same size mince as the shiitakes. Do not puree! Transfer to a mixing bowl and combine with the napa cabbage, chives, ginger, and tamari or soy sauce.

To prepare the potstickers, have a small bowl of water, your filling, and a tablespoon nearby, as well as wonton wrappers and a large parchment-lined baking sheet.

Place 3 wrappers onto the baking sheet. Scoop 1 tablespoon of the filling into the center of each wrapper. Dab water around the edge of the wrapper with your finger. Fold one side of the wrapper over the filling to create a half moon shape, then grab the edges and bring them to the top, while creating a flat bottom on the dumpling by gently pressing down on the filling. Pinch-pleat the edges at the top down to the bottom corners to seal. Slightly turn the corners inward. Repeat with the remaining filling and wrappers. At this point, you can freeze the sheet, and once the potstickers are frozen, transfer them to a freezer-safe container or bag. If you have leftover wrappers, you can freeze them also. Thaw in the fridge before using again.

When ready to cook the potstickers, place the sesame seeds on a small plate. Bring a pot of water to a boil and cook 6 to 8 potstickers at a time in the boiling water, until they start to float to the top, about 2 minutes. If boiling from frozen, boil for 3 to 4 minutes. With a slotted spoon, transfer the dumplings to a baking sheet or large plate.

Meanwhile, heat a large nonstick pan over medium heat with 1 teaspoon of the oil. Using a pair of tongs to hold the potsticker, place the flat bottom side into the plate of sesame seeds, generously coating it. Place the sesame seed side down into the hot pan and fry for about 4 minutes. You can turn the potstickers onto one side and fry for another 30 seconds to 1 minute if you feel the seam needs to be cooked and steamed a little. Fry in batches of 5 or 6 depending on how large your pan is, adding 1 teaspoon oil per batch.

Serve immediately, with sesame soy vinaigrette on the side for dipping.

FRIES & SALAD

 25 mins.   50 mins.

use Tahini Caesar Dressing (page 200) or any dressing of your choice

FRIES

4	russet potatoes
2	tablespoons avocado oil, olive oil, or neutral vegetable oil
1	teaspoon Old Bay Seasoning
½	teaspoon chipotle chili powder
½	teaspoon sea salt
½	teaspoon ground black pepper

SALAD

3	cups mesclun greens
2	cups coarsely chopped romaine lettuce
1	cup sliced English cucumber (about half a cucumber)
4	cocktail tomatoes or ½ cup cherry tomatoes, halved
1	avocado, diced
¼	cup thinly sliced red onion
¼	cup sliced kalamata olives
⅓	cup crumbled vegan feta (optional)
½	cup Tahini Caesar Dressing or any dressing of your choice

MAKES 2 SERVINGS It's the meal that ALL vegans know too well. We have ordered it, or been forced to order it, when eating out with friends at a place that doesn't accommodate vegans. If only restaurants really knew how we wanted our fries and salad, right? There's nothing sadder than seeing these two wonderful things arrive flaccid and unstyled, like two lame side dishes. Don't get me wrong—I love fries and salad. They make the perfect couple, good and bad, health food and junk food, yin and yang. It's the perfect balance! But there's a right way and wrong way to do it. Everyone else is doing it wrong so I had to make it right. My salad is kinda Greek style 'cause I like salty and crunchy stuff, and I could never get tired of eating homemade potato wedges. I hope this recipe does right by you, and if you've never tried fries on your salad, welcome to utopia!

Preheat the oven to 450°F. Line a large baking sheet with a Silpat mat or parchment paper. (I find Silpat works really well for roasting and crisping potatoes evenly.)

To make the fries, wash the potatoes. Cut each potato in half lengthwise and then cut each half lengthwise on a diagonal into equal-sized wedges.

Place the wedges in a large pot of cold water over high heat and bring to a simmer. Cook until you can just prick the surface with a fork and the potatoes are still somewhat firm.

Drain and immediately add the potatoes back to the pot. Toss with the oil, Old Bay, chili powder, sea salt, and black pepper and coat evenly.

Lay the potato wedges onto the prepared baking sheet, slightly spaced apart. Bake for 20 minutes, then flip and bake for 20 more minutes, until really golden brown and crispy.

Only dress the greens if you're eating them immediately. I like to toss the greens and romaine in 2 to 3 tablespoons of dressing and then top it with cucumber, tomatoes, avocado, red onion, olives plus the potato wedges, vegan feta, and more dressing on top.

the bowl bible

Making bowls full of variety that are actually satisfying seems easy, but truthfully I've found it to be quite an art to make them *really* good. And I'll tell you what else: those pay-by-weight sorry excuses for salad bar places have nothing on homemade…AND you'll save a lot of dollars too!

Here's my formula for
creating the perfect bowls:

1. Start with a complex-carby grain base.
2. Use all the raw veg your heart desires
   (you can handle that!).
3. But to make a bowl comforting, it needs to
   be mixed with cooked veg too.
4. One or two hearty additions bringing protein
   and texture are going to fill ya up and give ya
   something satisfying to chew.
5. A creamy dressing will take your bowl over
   the top, and I deal almost exclusively with them.
   Try my Salad Dressings for Dummies (page 198)
   and add some satiating fat to the party!
6. Top the bowl with a couple (or maybe a few)
   kinds of toasted nuts & seeds—sunflower seeds,
   chopped walnuts, chopped pistachios,
   almonds, pumpkin seeds, hemp hearts,
   or sesame seeds.

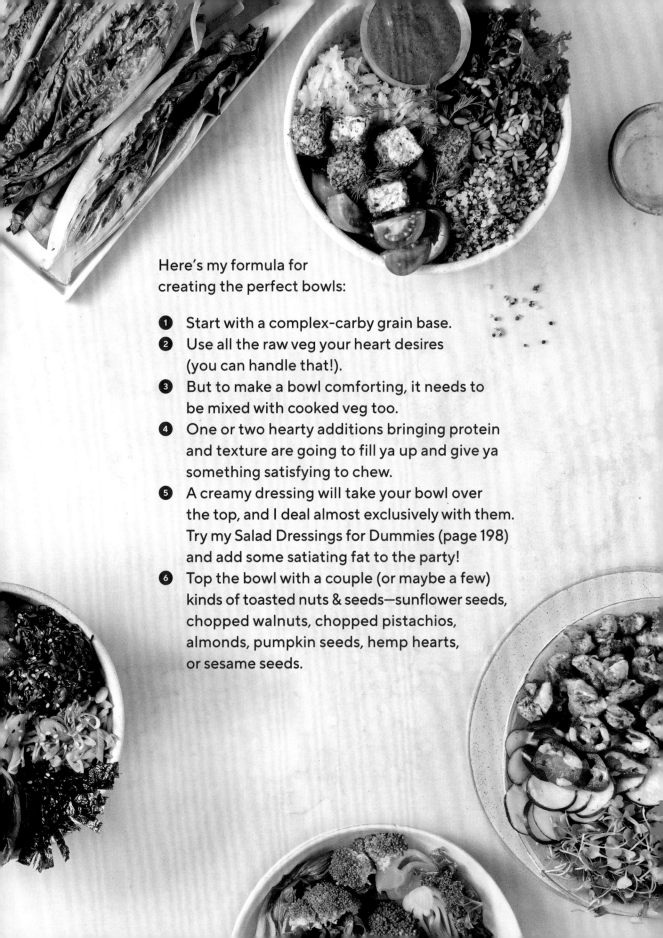

GRAIN BASES

MAKES 4 SERVINGS OF EACH Just like building anything, ya gotta start with a good foundation! Here are my favorite grain bases to start making the perfect bowl. You can prepare these in advance, according to the package instructions, and refrigerate them for up to 5 days.

2½ cups cooked buckwheat groats
(1 cup/6.5 oz/185 g dried grain)

3 cups cooked quinoa
(1 cup/6.35 oz/180 g dried grain)

2½ cups cooked farro
(1 cup/6.8 oz/192 g dried grain)

4 cups cooked short-grain brown rice
(1 cup/8.5 oz/240 g dried grain)

4 cups cooked soba noodles
(8 oz/230 g dried)

COOKED VEG

You will of course add some raw veg to your perfect bowl, but I insist on adding in some uniquely cooked vegetables, too! These all hold up pretty well after being cooked, so don't worry if you wanna meal-prep them at the start of the week. Store each in separate containers in the fridge. Unless otherwise mentioned, most will be OK for up to 5 days; reheat before topping on your bowl.

ROASTED PURPLE CABBAGE SLAW

GRILLED ROMAINE HEARTS

STEAMED KALE, BOK CHOY & BROCCOLI

BLISTERED TOMATOES

ROASTED CURRY CAULIFLOWER

GRILLED ROMAINE HEARTS

 1 min.   6 mins.

MAKES 2 ROMAINE HEARTS / 4 SERVINGS This one is really best eaten immediately, as when it's served warm on your grain bowl, it's just delicious. But the grilled romaine is still OK if eaten one day later in a meal-prepped salad. I also like it assembled as its own fancy Caesar salad, topped with **Crunchy Butter Beans (page 96)** instead of croutons and more Tahini Caesar Dressing.

use Tahini Caesar Dressing (page 200)

INGREDIENTS

2   romaine hearts, sliced in half lengthwise

1   tablespoon Tahini Caesar Dressing

Place a cast-iron grill pan over high heat. Brush each half of the romaine hearts with tahini Caesar dressing on the cut side. When the pan is hot, place 2 halved hearts in the pan, cut-side-down. Grill for 2 to 3 minutes, until they char. Transfer to a plate. Lower the heat to medium and repeat with the other 2 halves. Brush with more dressing on the grilled side when serving.

ROASTED PURPLE CABBAGE SLAW

 10 mins.   20 mins.

MAKES ABOUT 4 CUPS Roasting purple cabbage makes it really easy to eat and enjoy! I like it pickled, too, but I'm a big fan of the less pungent flavor it gets from cooking this way. The cabbage should be shredded on a mandoline or box grater to get the best texture.

INGREDIENTS

8   cups shredded purple cabbage

2   tablespoons olive oil or avocado oil

1   teaspoon sea salt

Preheat the oven to 425°F.

Spread out the cabbage onto 2 large baking sheets in an even layer.

Divide the oil and sea salt among both batches and use your hands to mix well. It will look like a lot of cabbage but will shrink when roasted.

Bake for 20 minutes, tossing the cabbage and swapping the baking sheets on the racks in the oven halfway through.

STEAMED KALE, BOK CHOY & BROCCOLI

 10 mins. 7–8 mins.

MAKES 4 SERVINGS These are my three fave veggies to steam so they're ready for all my bowl-making needs!

INGREDIENTS

2   cups broccoli florets (about 1 broccoli crown)
4   baby bok choy heads, sliced in half lengthwise
2½   cups packed curly kale, large stem removed and torn into pieces (about 1 small bunch)

Place a steamer basket inside a large stockpot and pour in 1 to 2 inches of water so it comes up to just below the bottom of the insert. Place the broccoli and bok choy in first and the kale at the top and place a lid on the pot.

Place the pot over medium-high heat, and once the water begins simmering, it will take only 3 minutes or so until the kale and bok choy are bright green and wilted and the broccoli is bright green and tender but still slightly crisp. Remove the vegetables from the pot immediately, and if eating right away, leave them warm. If you're meal prepping and storing these for later, place all the vegetables into a colander and run cold water over them for 30 seconds to 1 minute to prevent further cooking. Before storing the veg in the fridge, allow the excess water to drain off.

BLISTERED TOMATOES

 1 min. 20 mins.

MAKES 2 CUPS Once you blister cherry or grape tomatoes, you won't ever go back to eating them raw. They're like little bursts of homemade marinara in your mouth and complement grain bowls or pastas of any kind.

INGREDIENTS

2   cups cherry or grape tomatoes (1 pint)

Preheat the oven to 450°F.

Add tomatoes onto a baking sheet and bake for 16 to 20 minutes, until they are shrunken and blistered with some browned charred marks.

ROASTED CURRY CAULIFLOWER

 10 mins. 20 mins.

MAKES 4 SERVINGS (ABOUT 3 CUPS) Raw cauli just ain't for me, no thank you! But roast it up with spices and I'll eat the whole dang head of it.

INGREDIENTS

1   tablespoon lemon juice (about half a lemon)
1   tablespoon olive oil or avocado oil
1   teaspoon yellow curry powder
1   teaspoon sea salt
1   head of cauliflower, cut into medium-size florets (about 6 cups)

Preheat the oven to 450°F.

In a small dish, combine the lemon juice, oil, curry powder, and sea salt. Add the cauliflower to a nonstick or parchment-lined baking sheet, pour the sauce on top, and use your hands to coat the florets evenly.

Roast for 18 to 20 minutes, flipping halfway, until you see some charring on the florets.

CRISPY TOFU FINGERS

HEARTY ADDITIONS

How are ya going to power up your bowl unless you have some hearty additions? These five bowl components are the MOST important players in the anatomy of the perfect bowl, as they pack in the protein and add the chewy, meaty, and comforting textures that are key when you're eating a lot of cooked or raw vegetables! Find your vice and chow down.

TEMPEH BACON CHUNKS

CRUNCHY BUTTER BEANS

MISO-ROASTED KABOCHA SQUASH

CHICKEN SHAWARMA

CRISPY TOFU FINGERS

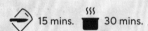 15 mins. 30 mins.

MAKES 8 FINGERS OR 16 CHUNKS I can eat tofu any and ALL ways, but I love breading and baking it like this. The technique gives it the same texture as chicken fingers, so it's perfect for adding a meaty component to your grain bowls. You're also going to be obsessed with them once you try the **HFF Famous Bowls (page 153)**, where they take center stage!

INGREDIENTS

1	brick (16 oz/450 g) medium-firm or firm tofu
½	cup multigrain or panko-style bread crumbs
2	teaspoons chili powder
2	teaspoons granulated garlic powder
1	teaspoon dried thyme
1	teaspoon dried oregano
1	teaspoon dried basil
1	teaspoon sea salt
½	teaspoon ground black pepper
2	tablespoons Dijon mustard
1	tablespoon unsweetened nondairy milk
	Vegetable oil spray, for baking

Preheat the oven to 425°F. Line a baking sheet with a Silpat mat or parchment paper.

Drain the tofu from the packaging water and pat dry with a clean tea towel. Cut into 8 thick sticks or fingers if eating as a snack or finger food. For use in the HFF famous bowls, you can cut those in half again for 16 chunks.

In a mixing bowl, combine the bread crumbs, chili powder, garlic powder, thyme, oregano, basil, sea salt, and black pepper.

In a small bowl, mix the Dijon with the nondairy milk until smooth and well combined.

Brush the Dijon mixture evenly on each piece of tofu, coating all sides well. Coat each piece fully in the bread crumb mixture. Place the breaded pieces on the prepared baking sheet.

Spray the pieces with a light coating of vegetable oil and bake for 30 minutes, flipping halfway through the bake time. They should be a deep golden brown.

Refrigerate leftovers and consume within 5 days. You can reheat pieces on a baking sheet in a 425°F oven for 5 to 10 minutes.

HOT TIP This recipe is easy to customize for different flavor profiles and purposes. If you don't have Dijon mustard for the coating, use hot sauce, hoisin, or another tasty condiment. You can also swap water for the nondairy milk. You can switch up the herbs and spices in the breading, use other types of bread crumbs, or add hemp hearts, ground flax, chia seeds, or other things to the bread crumbs for extra nutrition or crunch. You can also cut the tofu into triangles or tear big chunks by hand for less uniform pieces. The options are endless!

HOT TIP You can use leftover roasted squash to make **Kabocha Stuffed Shells (page 130)**, **Kabocha Wonton Ravioli with Miso Butter (page 132)**, and **Kabocha Broth with Udon (page 135)**.

MISO-ROASTED KABOCHA SQUASH

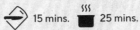 15 mins. 25 mins.

MAKES 4 TO 6 SERVINGS I love kabocha so much— it's my number-one squash! It's a Japanese variety of pumpkin, but be sure not to confuse it with buttercup squash. They're sometimes even mixed up and/or mislabeled at grocery stores, but once you've tasted both, you'll agree that the flavor and texture of kabocha is much better. Your best bet for finding it is at larger grocery stores and Asian grocers or produce markets. You can even eat the peel of this superior squash! My affection for roasted kabocha is so endless that I've created three more ways you can use the leftovers for delish dinner stuff.

INGREDIENTS

- 2½–3 pound kabocha squash
- 1 tablespoon toasted sesame oil
- 1 tablespoon gluten-free tamari or low-sodium soy sauce
- 1 teaspoon mellow white miso
- ¼ teaspoon Chinese five spice powder
- ¼ teaspoon sea salt
- ¼ teaspoon ground black pepper

Preheat the oven to 450°F.

To prepare the kabocha squash, use a sharp, sturdy knife to cut the squash in half. Scoop out the seeds and discard. Place the flat side of each half down and cut into ¾-inch thick wedges.

In a small mixing bowl, combine the sesame oil, tamari or soy sauce, miso, five spice powder, sea salt, and black pepper.

Place all the squash pieces onto a large baking sheet. Drizzle the miso mixture on top and use your hands and the bottom of the baking sheet to coat all sides of the squash. Spread out the pieces in an even layer, slightly spaced apart.

Bake the squash for 20 to 25 minutes, flipping half-way through, until roasted and dark golden brown in spots.

CRUNCHY BUTTER BEANS

 5 mins.   35 mins.

MAKES 1 CUP These crunchy beans are going to be so good in your bowls, but I suspect you'll love them so much you'll probably want to snack on 'em, too!

INGREDIENTS

1   can (15 oz/439 g) butter beans, drained and rinsed (about 1⅓ cups)
1   tablespoon olive oil or avocado oil
1   teaspoon ground cumin
½   teaspoon smoked paprika
½   teaspoon sea salt
½   teaspoon ground black pepper
¼   teaspoon cayenne pepper

Preheat the oven to 425°F. Line a baking sheet with a Silpat mat or parchment paper.

If there are any outer skins easily coming off in your batch of beans, remove and discard them. Toss the beans in the olive oil, cumin, smoked paprika, sea salt, black pepper, and cayenne until evenly coated.

Spread out onto the prepared baking sheet in one even layer. Bake for 30 to 35 minutes, flipping once halfway through, until golden brown and crispy.

Store leftovers in a container in a cool, dry place and consume within 3 or 4 days.

CHICKEN SHAWARMA

 15 mins. 10 mins. soaking 🍲 20 mins.

MAKES 4 SERVINGS Soy curls are one of the best vegan meat substitutes. Butler Foods makes them from whole soy beans and then dehydrates them, so they can take on any flavor and are the perfect chewy texture to mimic chicken or beef. They're also full of protein and fiber and therefore very filling…you only need a small portion! There're so many vegan grocery and supply stores online now that you can order them from if you can't find them at your local health or specialty food store. We use them a few more times in this cookbook—whenever they're called for, you can substitute with unbreaded vegan chicken pieces; just skip the soaking.

INGREDIENTS

2	cups dried soy curls or vegan chicken pieces
2	tablespoons olive oil
1	tablespoon vegan chicken-flavored bouillon or vegetable bouillon or 1 cube
2	teaspoons apple cider vinegar
2	teaspoons granulated garlic powder
2	teaspoons onion powder
2	teaspoons dried oregano
1	teaspoon ground cumin
1	teaspoon ground black pepper
½	teaspoon ground turmeric

Preheat the oven to 425°F. Line a baking sheet with a Silpat mat or parchment paper.

Add the soy curls to a bowl and cover with water. Let them soak for 5 to 10 minutes, until expanded. (If using vegan chicken pieces, you can skip this step.) Using your hands, squeeze the moisture out of the soy curls and reserve 2 tablespoons of the soaking liquid.

In a bowl, combine the reserved soaking liquid (if using vegan chicken pieces, add 2 tablespoons fresh water), olive oil, vegan bouillon, apple cider vinegar, garlic powder, onion powder, oregano, cumin, black pepper, and turmeric until well combined. Toss the soy curls in this sauce until well coated.

Spread the soy curls in an even layer on the prepared baking sheet. Bake for 18 to 20 minutes, flipping halfway through, until golden and browned in spots. The soy curls will feel a bit soft out of the oven but will get chewier as they cool, so be sure you don't overbake them.

Store leftovers in the fridge and consume within 7 days.

TEMPEH BACON CHUNKS

 10 mins. 30 mins.

MAKES 2 CUPS I couldn't make a cookbook without a bacony staple, so enter Tempeh Bacon Chunks! This is like the bacon marinade in my first cookbook, with a couple of new additions like nutritional yeast and garlic powder. I only use chunks or crumbles throughout the recipes in this book, but you could also cut your tempeh brick into thin slices about ⅛ inch thick and get those crispy in the oven for sandwiches or wraps. You'll see many ways to use this recipe throughout the book, such as in **Zuppa Toscana (page 62)**, **Zucchini Carbonara (page 146)**, and a lot of the breakfast stuff.

INGREDIENTS

2	tablespoons gluten-free tamari or low-sodium soy sauce
1	tablespoon avocado oil or neutral vegetable oil
1	tablespoon maple syrup
½	tablespoon liquid smoke
½	tablespoon nutritional yeast
½	teaspoon smoked paprika
½	teaspoon garlic powder
1	brick (8 oz/227 g) tempeh (about 2 cups crumbled)
	Sea salt, to taste

Preheat the oven to 425°F. Line a baking sheet with a Silpat mat or parchment paper.

In a mixing bowl, combine the tamari or soy sauce, oil, maple syrup, liquid smoke, nutritional yeast, smoked paprika, and garlic powder.

Using your hands, tear the tempeh into small chunks directly into the marinade and toss to coat evenly.

If you're using this in the Zuppa Toscana or Zucchini Carbonara, head on over to those pages to make the rest of the dish. You will not bake the tempeh for those recipes.

Otherwise, lay out the marinated tempeh chunks on the prepared baking sheet in one even layer, with chunks slightly spaced apart. Bake for 25 to 30 minutes, flipping halfway through the bake time, until drier-looking, golden brown, and slightly caramelized on the edges. Sprinkle with the sea salt.

Store leftovers in the fridge and consume within 10 days.

GRILLED CHEESE 4 WAYS

You're about to enter vegan grilled cheese heaven! While I probably could come up with eight more grilled cheese concoctions for ya, I thought four was plenty abundant to get you started. And besides, once you get the hang of melting that vegan cheese, I leave the creativity up to you. What I hope is that my mash-ups will get your imagination flowing and your stomach growling!

THE "SHARP" GRILLED CHEESE

THE "SPICED" GRILLED CHEESE

THE "SWEET" GRILLED CHEESE

THE "CREAMY" GRILLED CHEESE

THE "SHARP" GRILLED CHEESE

 10 mins. 33 mins.

MAKES 2 SANDWICHES This sharp and tangy grilled cheese sandwich comes stuffed with buttery caramelized onions, thinly sliced green apple, and a sharp vegan Cheddar! Of course, if you can't find the same cheese I'm using, whatever your fave is will do, too. You could even use a soft, spreadable cashew cheese infused with garlic and herbs.

CARAMELIZED ONIONS (MAKES ½ CUP)

2	tablespoons vegan butter
2½	cups thinly sliced onion (about 1 onion)
1	teaspoon sea salt

GRILLED CHEESE

2	tablespoons vegan butter, softened to room temperature
4	large slices sourdough bread
6	slices vegan medium or mature Cheddar
1	Granny Smith apple, sliced thin (about 20 slices)

To caramelize the onion, heat a nonstick pan with vegan butter over medium heat. Once the butter is melted and sizzling, add the onion and sea salt and toss to coat well. Cook for 8 to 10 minutes, stirring occasionally, until the onion starts to turn light brown. Turn the heat down to medium-low and cook for another 12 to 14 minutes, stirring regularly to evenly brown.

To make the grilled cheese, spread ½ tablespoon of the room-temp vegan butter on the outside of each slice of bread. On the inside of one slice of bread, add 3 slices of cheese, 9 or 10 apple slices, and half the caramelized onions. Top with the slice of bread with butter on the outside. Repeat with the second sandwich.

Heat a large nonstick pan over medium-low heat. Cook one sandwich at a time in the same pan and place a lid on top. Fry for 3 to 5 minutes, until golden brown. Flip the sandwich and fry the other side, covered, for another 2 to 3 minutes, until golden brown. On the second side you will probably need to lower the heat, as the pan is now hotter. You can turn the burner off and leave the lid on for another minute to melt the cheese further, if needed. The lid is necessary to melt the vegan cheese properly! Repeat with the second sandwich. Let the sandwich rest for a couple of minutes before slicing with a sharp knife.

THE "SPICED" GRILLED CHEESE

 10 mins. 15 mins.

MAKES 2 SANDWICHES Stuffing the roasted curry cauliflower into a grilled cheese was a total home run! The spice complements the sweet homemade mango chutney so well. You can use any remaining mango chutney in bowls or **My Everyday Roasted Vegetable Salad (page 76)**, but I'm sure you'll find other uses for it, too! You can swap the granulated sugar for brown sugar or coconut sugar in the chutney, but the final product will be darker in color.

use leftover Roasted Curry Cauliflower (page 89)

MANGO CHUTNEY (MAKES ¾ CUP)

1¼	cups frozen mango chunks
⅓	cup white or apple cider vinegar
¼	cup granulated sugar
1	tablespoon minced garlic (about 2 large cloves)
1	tablespoon raisins or dried currants
½	teaspoon peeled and grated fresh ginger
½	teaspoon ground coriander
½	teaspoon sea salt
¼	teaspoon chili flakes
¼	teaspoon ground cinnamon
⅛	teaspoon ground nutmeg

GRILLED CHEESE

2	tablespoons vegan butter, softened to room temperature
4	large slices sourdough bread
6	slices vegan smoked gouda or Cheddar
1¼	cups leftover Roasted Curry Cauliflower florets

To make the mango chutney, add the mango, vinegar, sugar, garlic, raisins, ginger, coriander, sea salt, chili flakes, cinnamon, and nutmeg to a saucepan over medium heat and bring to a simmer. Lower the heat and simmer for 10 to 12 minutes, until reduced and thickened. If your mango chunks are too big, once they soften, break them up with a fork or potato masher right in the pot while they cook. Let the mango chutney cool before using in the grilled cheese.

To make the grilled cheese, spread ½ tablespoon of the vegan butter on the outside of each slice of bread. Spread 2 to 3 tablespoons of mango chutney on the inside of one slice of bread, next layer 3 slices of cheese and add about half the roasted curry cauliflower florets. Top with the slice of bread with butter on the outside. Repeat with the second sandwich.

Heat a large nonstick pan over medium-low heat. Cook one sandwich at a time in the same pan and place a lid on top. Fry for 3 to 5 minutes, until golden brown. Flip the sandwich and fry the other side, covered, for another 2 to 3 minutes, until golden brown. On the second side you will probably need to lower the heat, as the pan is now hotter. You can turn the burner off and leave the lid on for another minute to melt the cheese further, if needed. The lid is necessary to melt the vegan cheese properly! Repeat with the second sandwich. Let the sandwich rest for a couple of minutes before slicing with a sharp knife.

THE "SWEET" GRILLED CHEESE

 10 mins. 10 mins.

MAKES 2 SANDWICHES Sweet cheese, this is a good sandwich, and is my favorite of all four grilled cheese offerings! I personally think sweet, fruity jam goes with tangy or smoky cheese, like gravy on mashed potatoes. You can't have one without the other. It must be done! I threw the crispy onion strings in there to break it up with a crunch, but I also think regular ol' chips could work, too. No, I'm not stoned.

use Crispy Onion Strings (page 194)

GRILLED CHEESE

2	tablespoons vegan butter, softened to room temperature
4	large slices sourdough bread
¼	cup seedless raspberry jam
6	slices vegan smoked gouda
20	Crispy Onion Strings

To make the grilled cheese, spread ½ tablespoon of the vegan butter on the outside of each slice of bread. Spread 1 tablespoon of jam on the inside of one slice of bread, and add 3 slices of cheese and 10 crispy onion strings. Top with the slice of bread with butter on the outside. Repeat with the second sandwich.

Heat a large nonstick pan over medium-low heat. Cook one sandwich at a time in the same pan and place a lid on top. Fry for 3 to 5 minutes, until golden brown. Flip the sandwich and fry the other side, covered, for another 2 to 3 minutes, until golden brown. On the second side you will probably need to lower the heat, as the pan is now hotter. You can turn the burner off and leave the lid on for another minute to melt the cheese further, if needed. The lid is necessary to melt the vegan cheese properly! Repeat with the second sandwich. Let the sandwich rest for a couple of minutes before slicing with a sharp knife.

THE "CREAMY" GRILLED CHEESE

 15 mins. 30 mins.

MAKES 2 SANDWICHES I'm glad I tried making tuna out of tempeh because the texture is perfect and I prefer it to chickpea tuna. That version has been on hotforfoodblog.com for a while, and you could still use that here if you prefer. This mock tuna is hearty, high in protein, tangy, sweet, and very much like the real thing. You can also make more of a classic tuna sandwich, too, on lightly toasted bread, and add fixins like lettuce, tomato, and extra pickle slices or skip the bread altogether and add the tempeh tuna to salads and grain bowls!

TEMPEH TUNA (MAKES 2½ CUPS)

1	brick (8 oz/227 g) tempeh, crumbled
2	cups low-sodium vegetable stock
1	teaspoon dulse granules
½	cup finely chopped celery
¼	cup finely chopped red onion
¼	cup finely chopped garlic dill pickle (1 pickle)
½	cup vegan mayonnaise
1	tablespoon Dijon mustard
1	tablespoon lemon juice (about half a lemon)
1	tablespoon finely chopped fresh dill
½	teaspoon sea salt
½	teaspoon ground black pepper

GRILLED CHEESE

2	tablespoons vegan butter, softened to room temperature
4	large slices sourdough bread
6	slices vegan medium or mature Cheddar

Combine the tempeh, vegetable stock, and dulse in a saucepan over high heat and bring to a boil. Reduce the heat and simmer for 20 minutes until all the liquid is gone. Remove the pot from the heat and let the tempeh cool. If there is any excess liquid in the tempeh once cooled, just strain it before adding the remaining ingredients.

Place the tempeh in a mixing bowl. Add the celery, onion, pickle, mayonnaise, Dijon, lemon juice, dill, sea salt, and black pepper and mix until well combined. You can refrigerate this and consume within 4 to 5 days.

To make the grilled cheese, spread ½ tablespoon of the vegan butter on the outside of each slice of bread. On the inside of one slice of bread, add 3 slices of cheese and half of the tempeh tuna. Top with the slice of bread with butter on the outside. Repeat with the second sandwich.

Heat a large nonstick pan over medium-low heat. Cook one sandwich at a time in the same pan and place a lid on top. Fry for 3 to 5 minutes, until golden brown. Flip the sandwich and fry the other side, covered, for another 2 to 3 minutes, until golden brown. On the second side you will probably need to lower the heat, as the pan is now hotter. You can turn the burner off and leave the lid on for another minute to melt the cheese further, if needed. The lid is necessary to melt the vegan cheese properly! Repeat with the second sandwich. Let the sandwich rest for a couple of minutes before slicing with a sharp knife.

You could also keep this sandwich open-faced and fry each slice of bread, butter side down, with cheese on top of the tempeh tuna, side by side in the pan.

dinner stuff

Dinner stuff is a little more filling, a little more stick-to-your-(vegan) ribs! Easy pastas are my fave for dinner, so there're lots of those recipes. Things like carbonara, ragu bolognese, ravioli, stuffed shells, and more. There's also stuff you might not have thought to have for dinner, like Buffalo Chicken Crunch Wraps, Korean BBQ Burritos, or Cauliflower Piccata. This is the kind of food you'll serve for dinner parties, date nights, and to feed the whole damn fam. I also put a lot of tastiness into a really easy one-pot mac n' cheese—pizza stuff, Thai stuff, green stuff, and buffalo wing stuff. One look at those pics and you'll be stuffed! But there's an added bonus: when the stuff is this good, you won't mind eating leftovers tomorrow.

ONE-POT MAC N' CHEESE

5 mins. 15 mins.

INGREDIENTS

1½	cups water
1	cup unsweetened nondairy milk
2	tablespoons nutritional yeast
1	tablespoon apple cider vinegar
2	teaspoons tomato paste
1	teaspoon Dijon mustard
1	teaspoon sea salt
	Pinch cayenne pepper (optional)
1⅔	cups elbow macaroni
¾	cup vegan Cheddar shreds
1	tablespoon vegan butter
	Ground black pepper, to taste

MAKES ABOUT 3 CUPS (3 SERVINGS) I had to level up my already-perfect versions of mac n' cheese! With so many ways to make the same thing, I can't stop myself. So I present to you the easiest mac n' cheese ever, and it's all made in one pot. This is the same vibe as what we Canadians know as KD (aka Kraft Dinner). Americans had the exact same product but it was labeled Kraft Macaroni & Cheese. I don't know why. This is obviously better and healthier, but it's channeling that era. Eat it straight up or level it up in a big way with my five extremely epic variations that follow.

In a pot over medium-high heat, add the water and nondairy milk and bring to a low simmer, 5 to 6 minutes, whisking occasionally to prevent burning. The mixture will get foamy.

Turn the heat down slightly to keep the liquid at a low simmer. Whisk in the nutritional yeast, apple cider vinegar, tomato paste, Dijon, sea salt, and cayenne, until well combined. Add the macaroni and stir. Cook the mixture over a low simmer, uncovered, for 7 to 8 minutes, until al dente. (Double-check your pasta's package directions because the cook time will vary depending on the brand and what the pasta is made from.) Stir the mixture constantly to prevent sticking.

When the pasta is done, the sauce will look a little thin. Take the pot off the heat and stir in the vegan Cheddar shreds, vegan butter, and black pepper. Cover the pot for 1 to 2 minutes and then stir with a wooden spoon until the sauce thickens up and the cheese is completely melted.

Serve with extra ground black pepper, if desired, or level up your mac n' cheese with one of the variations that follow. To reheat leftovers, add 1 to 2 tablespoons of nondairy milk and heat over medium-low until warmed through.

15 mins.   20 mins.

C 10 mins. soaking

BUFFALO CHICKEN MAC N' CHEESE

use One-Pot Mac n' Cheese (page 110)

Jalapeño Ranch (page 190)

MAKES ABOUT 4 CUPS (ABOUT 3 SERVINGS) This leveled-up mac is hot and spicy! It's mac smashed with buffalo chicken and I even included the celery, carrots, and ranch that you'd get on the side of your order of hot wings. This all works together for one awesome smorgasbord of seriously addictive mac n' cheese. If you double the amount of soy curls, coat them all in the sauce, and bake them the same way, they'll be ready to make the **Buffalo Chicken Crunch Wraps (page 142)**—or try putting this whole damn thing IN the crunch wrap...oh hell yeah!

INGREDIENTS

1 cup dried soy curls

½ cup buffalo-style hot sauce

3 tablespoons melted vegan butter

2 tablespoons apple cider vinegar

1 tablespoon finely chopped fresh dill

2 teaspoons vegan chicken-flavored bouillon base or 1 cube

1 teaspoon onion powder

1 teaspoon granulated garlic powder

½ teaspoon chipotle chili powder

½ teaspoon sea salt

½ teaspoon ground black pepper

¼ cup finely chopped chives, divided

1 batch One-Pot Mac n' Cheese

½ cup finely diced carrot (about 1 small carrot)

½ cup finely diced celery (about 1 stalk)

1 batch Jalapeño Ranch

Preheat the oven to 425°F. Line a baking sheet with a Silpat mat or parchment paper.

Put the dried soy curls in a bowl and pour water over them until covered. Let the soy curls hydrate and expand for about 10 minutes. Before draining the soy curls, reserve 2 teaspoons of the soaking liquid. Drain the soy curls in a fine-mesh sieve, squeezing out excess water.

In the same bowl, combine the reserved soaking liquid, hot sauce, melted vegan butter, apple cider vinegar, dill, bouillon base, onion powder, garlic powder, chili powder, sea salt, black pepper, and 2 tablespoons of the chives. Reserve half the sauce for serving. Add the drained soy curls to the remaining sauce and toss with a spatula to coat evenly.

Transfer the soy curls to the prepared baking sheet. Bake for 18 to 20 minutes, flipping halfway through, until golden and browned in spots.

Fold half of the carrot and celery into the prepared mac n' cheese, reserving the rest for garnish.

Top each serving with the baked buffalo soy curls, the remaining buffalo sauce, and the jalapeño ranch, and garnish with the remaining carrot, celery, and chives.

HOT TIP Feel free to use some of the pizza sauce from this recipe to make the **One-Pot Mac n' Cheese** recipe, instead of tomato paste.

PIZZA MAC N' CHEESE

 10 mins. 12 mins.

use One-Pot Mac n' Cheese (page 110)

INGREDIENTS

1	package (4.2 oz/120 g) vegan pepperoni (about 44 slices)
½	cup finely diced red onion
1	batch One-Pot Mac n' Cheese
½	cup finely diced green bell pepper
2	tablespoons finely chopped fresh basil, plus more for garnish
1	tablespoon finely chopped fresh oregano
¼	cup store-bought pizza sauce

MAKES ABOUT 4 CUPS (3 SERVINGS) While I was dreaming of what else to smash together with mac n' cheese, pizza was an obvious contender. Their anatomy is the same—cheese, sauce, and carbs. No-brainer! The only thing missing here is the crust. But it's not necessary when all the pizza flavor from the onion, vegan pepperoni, green pepper, basil, and oregano stands out even while you shovel it into your face.

Preheat the oven to 425°F. Line a large baking sheet with a Silpat mat or parchment paper.

Lay out the pepperoni slices on the baking sheet slightly touching and fill the rest of the baking sheet with the diced onion in an even layer. Bake for 12 to 13 minutes, flipping halfway through, until the pepperoni gets slightly toasted and the onion is soft.

Add the pepperoni and onion to the prepared mac n' cheese, along with the green pepper, basil, and oregano. Stir to combine well.

Drizzle with the pizza sauce and garnish with more basil before serving.

THAI RED CURRY MAC N' CHEESE

 15 mins. 10 mins.

*use One-Pot Mac n' Cheese
(page 110)*

INGREDIENTS

1	teaspoon vegetable oil
1	package (8 oz/227 g) unbreaded vegan chicken pieces (about 1¾ cups)
¼	teaspoon sea salt
¼	teaspoon ground white pepper or ground black pepper
½	cup canned full-fat coconut milk
2	tablespoons Thai red curry paste (add 1 more tablespoon for hot)
2	tablespoons lime juice (about 1 large lime)
1	tablespoon mellow white miso
1½	teaspoons lime zest (about 1 large lime)
1	batch One-Pot Mac n' Cheese
1	cup fresh baby spinach
½	cup coarsely chopped fresh cilantro
2	tablespoons coarsely chopped Thai basil (optional)
½	teaspoon granulated garlic powder
¼	teaspoon chili powder
⅔	cup bean sprouts (optional)
¼	cup roasted salted peanuts or cashews, finely chopped or crushed

MAKES 5 CUPS (4 SERVINGS) This one's the boldest of the bunch and might seem a little strange on paper, but trust me when I say it's distinctive, sophisticated, and wicked tasty. Most curry pastes I've found are vegan friendly, but look out for shrimp paste or fish sauce in the list of ingredients. Those would be a no-go! Otherwise everything else in this recipe is straightforward. You could also swap the vegan chicken pieces for soy curls or tofu, of course. You'd just need to soak and drain the soy curls (see page 113).

Heat a cast-iron or nonstick pan over medium heat and add the oil and vegan chicken pieces. Season with sea salt and pepper. Cook for 2 to 3 minutes on each side, until browned.

While the chicken is browning, in a bowl, combine the coconut milk, curry paste, lime juice, miso, and lime zest until smooth. Add to the pan and coat the vegan chicken pieces, scraping up any brown bits that have formed at the bottom of the pan. Cook until the liquid reduces and thickens slightly, 3 to 5 minutes.

Add the chicken mixture to the prepared mac n' cheese, along with the spinach, cilantro, Thai basil, garlic powder, and chili powder. Stir to combine well. Serve topped with bean sprouts and chopped peanuts or cashews.

TEX-MEX MAC N' CHEESE

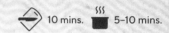 10 mins.   5–10 mins.

*use One-Pot Mac n' Cheese
(page 110)*

Cilantro Sour Cream (page 189)

INGREDIENTS

1	cup frozen or fresh corn kernels
1	batch One-Pot Mac n' Cheese
1	cup finely chopped green bell pepper
¾	cup canned black beans, drained and rinsed
1	tablespoon lime juice (about half a lime)
1	teaspoon chili powder
½	cup red salsa
½	cup Cilantro Sour Cream (or store-bought vegan sour cream)
¾	cup crushed tortilla chips

MAKES ABOUT 5 CUPS (ABOUT 4 SERVINGS) OK, partners, this is a little like mac n' cheese and nachos had a baby. And it's a hefty one! Ya gotta throw those tortilla chips on top or it's incomplete. Don't be shy, just go for it! You're hot for food, aren't you? I can't believe I didn't do this, but you could definitely use the tortilla strips from the **Tortilla Soup (page 46)** in place of the chips. I myself don't like to waste, so I just threw the crumbs from the bottom of the chip bag on top!

If using frozen corn, add to a bowl and cover with hot water. Let sit for 3 to 4 minutes and drain well.

To the prepared mac n' cheese, add the corn, green pepper, black beans, lime juice, and chili powder. Stir to combine well.

To serve, dollop with salsa, drizzle with cilantro sour cream or another vegan sour cream, and sprinkle with crushed tortilla chips.

GREEN MAC N' CHEESE

 5 mins. 10 mins.

*use One-Pot Mac n' Cheese
(page 110)*

INGREDIENTS

1   cup frozen or fresh peas

1   batch One-Pot Mac n' Cheese

1   cup packed mixed greens, coarsely chopped (such as arugula, spinach, baby kale)

2   tablespoons finely chopped fresh basil, divided

2   tablespoons store-bought vegan pesto, plus more for drizzling

⅓   cup salted shelled pistachios, coarsely chopped

MAKES 4 CUPS (ABOUT 3 SERVINGS) Pesto and pasta are two peas in a pod, so to do a variation with mac n' cheese isn't really a stretch. But I bulked up this simple idea with other yummy green things, like peas, so that you feel like the epitome of health eating it. It's also got mixed greens, 'cause we all need more of those, and chopped pistachios for a crunchy green addition on top. She's the prettiest of the group and you're going to be very fond of her.

If using frozen peas, add to a bowl and cover with hot water. Let sit for 3 to 4 minutes and drain well.

To the prepared mac n' cheese, add the peas, mixed greens, and half the basil. Stir to combine well.

Gently fold in the 2 tablespoons vegan pesto so it ribbons through the mac n' cheese. Top each serving with another drizzle of pesto, and sprinkle with the remaining basil and chopped pistachios.

RAGU BOLOGNESE

🍳 10 mins. ♨ 45 mins.

INGREDIENTS

- 1   white onion, peeled and coarsely chopped
- 2   carrots, coarsely chopped
- 1   celery stalk, coarsely chopped
- 1   pound cremini/baby bella mushrooms
- 2   zucchini, peeled and coarsely chopped
- 2   tablespoons olive oil
- 1   tablespoon minced garlic (2 or 3 large cloves)
- 1   teaspoon sea salt
- ⅓   cup tomato paste
- 1   tablespoon vegan beef-flavored bouillon base or mushroom bouillon base or 2 cubes
- ½   cup unsweetened soy or cashew milk
- 2   teaspoons balsamic vinegar
- 1   package (16 oz/454 g) pappardelle
- 1   tablespoon vegan butter
- 1   cup shredded vegan Parmesan, divided
-      Ground black pepper, to taste
-      Finely chopped fresh parsley, for garnish (optional)

HOT TIP You can substitute 1 tablespoon of vegan Worcestershire for the vegan beef-flavored or mushroom bouillon base.

MAKES 4 TO 6 SERVINGS Everyone has gotta have a good go-to bolognese recipe in their back pocket, and this is mine. A classic ragu bolognese is not a super tomatoey-saucy sauce, as it's made with ground meat and its juices. I used mushrooms because they're superior to meat and just as juicy! Sure, there's usually red wine in the base of the bolognese, but I made the executive decision to not do that—you can also tweak this to your liking. It's also traditional to use a flat pasta like pappardelle or tagliatelle, and you want to kiss and coat the noodles, not drown them in sauce!

In a large food processor, add the onion, carrot, and celery. Pulse blend until finely minced and set aside in a bowl. You should have 2 to 2¼ cups of this mixture.

Add the mushrooms and zucchini to the processor bowl. Pulse blend until finely minced and nearly a puree, then set aside in another bowl. You should have 4 to 4½ cups of this mixture.

In a large cast-iron pan or Dutch oven over medium heat, add the olive oil and the onion, carrot, and celery mixture. Sauté for about 5 minutes, until shrunk to about half. Add the garlic and sea salt and cook for another minute. Add the mushroom and zucchini mixture and cook for 15 to 18 minutes, stirring occasionally, until it looks more brown than green or gray and most of the water has been cooked out and you really can't distinguish the vegetables.

Add the tomato paste and bouillon base and cook for 3 to 5 more minutes, until it starts to caramelize. If you wanted to add in a splash of red wine, here's where you would do it and just cook a little longer.

Add the soy or cashew milk and balsamic vinegar and deglaze the pan, scraping up any brown bits at the bottom. Turn the heat down to low and simmer for another 10 minutes or so while your pasta cooks.

Meanwhile, bring a large pot of salted water to a boil and cook the pasta to al dente. Reserve 1 cup of the pasta cooking water and add it along with the vegan butter and ½ cup of the shredded vegan Parmesan to the sauce mixture. Stir to combine until the cheese is mostly melted, about 2 minutes, and then use tongs to

add the cooked pasta right into the pot of sauce. Use the tongs to coat the pasta properly, 1 to 2 minutes, until heated through and all the Parmesan is melted.

Serve the bolognese topped with the remaining vegan Parmesan, black pepper, and parsley.

EASY BRUSSELS SPROUTS PASTA

20 mins. ~~~ 25 mins.

INGREDIENTS

1	package (14 oz/400 g) linguine
½	cup raw walnuts
3–4	tablespoons olive oil, divided
1	pound brussels sprouts, trimmed and halved
½	cup sundried tomatoes (not oil packed), thinly sliced
¼	cup finely chopped shallot (about 1 shallot)
2	tablespoons minced garlic (3 or 4 large cloves)
2	teaspoons fresh thyme
⅓	cup dry white wine
2	tablespoons nutritional yeast
2	tablespoons lemon juice (about 1 lemon)
1–2	teaspoons lemon zest (about 1 lemon)
	Sea salt and ground black pepper, to taste
½	cup shredded vegan Parmesan, for garnish

MAKES 4 SERVINGS This pasta has always been a tried-and-true go-to. I usually just eyeball the whole thing, so I'm glad it's finally documented and can become part of your regular rotation, too! The sauce is light and simple, using shallots, garlic, white wine, lemon juice and zest, nutritional yeast, and pasta water. Don't overcook your brussels, because you want them bright and bursting with color. A cast-iron pan is best for preparing this dish to get that beautiful char on the brussels that other pans just won't accomplish.

Bring a large pot of salted water to a boil. Cook the linguine to al dente. Reserve ¼ cup of the pasta cooking water and set aside. Drain the pasta, but do not rinse.

While the pasta is cooking, heat a large cast-iron pan over medium-high heat and toast the walnuts for 4 to 5 minutes, until fragrant. Remove the walnuts from the pan and remove the pan from the heat to cool. Coarsely chop the walnuts and set aside.

Heat the same pan over medium heat with 2 tablespoons of the olive oil. Add the brussels sprouts cut-side-down and spread out into an even layer. Cook for 3 to 4 minutes without touching to allow them to get nicely browned. Toss once so the other side gets color, and cook for another 2 to 3 minutes. Transfer the brussels to a dish and set aside.

Lower the heat to medium-low and ensure the skillet isn't too hot from browning the brussels. If the pan is very dry, you can add another drizzle of olive oil or a bit of stock or water to the pan. Sauté the sundried tomatoes, shallot, garlic, and thyme. Stir to combine well and cook for another 3 to 4 minutes, tossing occasionally and adjusting the heat as necessary so the garlic doesn't burn.

Add the wine and simmer for another 3 to 4 minutes, tossing occasionally. Add the nutritional yeast, lemon juice, lemon zest, and remaining 1 tablespoon olive oil. Toss to combine and cook for another 2 to 3 minutes.

Add the linguine and toss everything until well combined. If the mixture looks dry, you can add the reserved pasta water and toss to combine. Toss the walnuts and brussels back in along with the sea salt and black pepper, to taste. Serve immediately, garnished with the vegan Parmesan.

HOT TIP Substitute the same amount of vegetable stock for the wine in this recipe. You could even add 1 teaspoon champagne vinegar or white wine vinegar to the stock to get the same effect.

BACON KALE PASTA

 10 mins.   20 mins.

*use Tempeh Bacon Chunks
(page 100)*

INGREDIENTS

1½	cups cherry or grape tomatoes
1	batch Tempeh Bacon Chunks
3	cups rotini pasta
2	cups packed lacinato kale, stemmed and finely chopped into ribbons
⅓	cup store-bought vegan pesto
¼	cup pitted kalamata olives, coarsely chopped
2	tablespoons lemon juice (about 1 lemon)
	Sea salt and ground black pepper, to taste
½	cup shredded vegan Parmesan, for garnish
½	cup toasted and salted pumpkin seeds, for garnish

MAKES 3 OR 4 SERVINGS This pasta is the epitome of my *What I Ate in a Day* vlogs. I eat this a lot! When I made this up in one of those videos, I snapped an ugly pic on my phone so I could remember to include the recipe in this cookbook. My intention is to bring you easy go-to meal ideas and stuff that you'd want to eat every week, and this dish is as #LaurenIRL as it gets!

Preheat the oven to 450°F.

Place the tomatoes on a baking sheet and bake for 16 to 20 minutes, until they are shrunken and blistered with some browned char marks. Remove from the oven and set aside.

Using another baking sheet, bake the marinated tempeh bacon chunks at the same time as the tomatoes. If your tempeh bacon is already made, just toss it on the baking sheet with the tomatoes in the last few minutes of cooking or reserve it to toss with the warm pasta.

Meanwhile, bring a large pot of salted water to a boil and cook the rotini until al dente. In the last minute of cooking, place the kale in the boiling water and let it wilt. Drain the pasta and kale, but do not rinse.

Add the pasta and kale back into the pot. Add the blistered tomatoes, tempeh bacon, pesto, olives, lemon juice, sea salt, and black pepper and toss until well combined. Garnish with vegan Parmesan and pumpkin seeds, and serve.

EASY TOFU & VEGGIE STIR-FRY

 20 mins.   30 mins.

*use Sesame Soy Vinaigrette
(page 201)*

INGREDIENTS

1	brick (16 oz/454 g) firm tofu
2	tablespoons neutral vegetable oil, for frying, plus a teaspoon
	Sea salt, to taste
1	package (12 oz/340 g) chow mein–style noodles
1	batch Sesame Soy Vinaigrette
1	tablespoon cornstarch (can substitute tapioca or arrowroot)
1	tablespoon agave nectar or granulated sugar
	Sriracha or chili garlic sauce, to taste (optional)
4	cups broccoli florets (1 large crown)
1	cup thinly sliced onion
1	cup sliced celery (about 2 stalks)
1	cup red bell pepper, cut into matchsticks (1 pepper)
1	tablespoon minced garlic (2 or 3 large cloves)
2	cups finely chopped napa cabbage
¼	cup finely chopped green onion (white and green parts), for garnish
1	tablespoon sesame seeds, for garnish

MAKES 4 SERVINGS This recipe accomplishes two things. First, it's your lesson in pan-frying crispy tofu cubes. I've been doing this for as long as I can remember, and people always ask how to do it. It's super simple; it just requires some patience. Don't be flipping too soon! Second, this stir-fry is a great fridge-cleaner at the end of the week. You can use any vegetables you have in your crisper before they go bad. You'll feel satisfied knowing you used that stuff up in time!

Squeeze the excess water from the brick of tofu using a clean tea towel. Cut into ½-inch cubes.

Heat a large nonstick pan over medium-high heat with the 2 table-spoons oil and fill the pan with the tofu cubes in one layer. You probably won't fit all the cubes at once. Once it starts frying, lower the heat slightly to medium. Fry on the first side for 8 to 9 minutes. You'll see a thin layer of crispy golden brown on the bottoms. Flip each cube gently with a fork to fry the other side for another 8 to 9 minutes. Once you flip the first batch, there will be room in the pan from the tofu shrinking, so you can add the remaining cubes and fry them for the same amount of time. Transfer the fried tofu to a plate, immediately sprinkle with sea salt, and set aside.

While the tofu is frying, cook the noodles according to the package directions. (Chow mein–style noodles come dried or precooked. Be careful not to overcook them, as you will stir-fry them as well.)

To transform the sesame soy vinaigrette into a stir-fry sauce, place I tablespoon of the vinaigrette in a small bowl. Add the cornstarch and agave and stir to combine into a slurry. Add this back into the remaining vinaigrette, combine well, and set aside. If you like your stir-fry sauce spicy, add sriracha or chili garlic sauce as well.

Heat the same large nonstick pan over medium-high heat. Add a teaspoon of the vegetable oil, if necessary; you might have enough residual oil from frying the tofu. Add the broccoli, onion, celery, red pepper, and garlic and sauté, stirring occasionally, for 9 to 10 minutes.

Add the drained noodles and cabbage or any other leafy veg you might be using, like kale, and stir to combine. Pour in all the stir-fry sauce, add the fried tofu, and toss with tongs to combine, cooking for another 2 minutes as the sauce thickens and coats everything.

Serve immediately, garnished with green onion and sesame seeds.

MISO-ROASTED KABOCHA SQUASH 3 WAYS

I have a feeling the miso-roasted kabocha squash from The Bowl Bible (page 95) is going to be one of your new fave meal staples. Aside from tossing it into bowls or salads, you can level up leftover squash into many other things. I'm going to share a few of the ways I transform it into tasty fillings and even a creamy broth!

KABOCHA STUFFED SHELLS

 20 mins.　50 mins.

use leftover Miso-Roasted Kabocha Squash (page 95)

TOFU RICOTTA (MAKES 3 CUPS)

1	brick (16 oz/454 g) firm or extra-firm tofu
¼	cup nutritional yeast
1	tablespoon minced garlic (2 to 3 large cloves)
1	tablespoon extra-virgin olive oil
1	tablespoon lemon juice (about half a lemon)
½	cup tightly packed fresh basil, finely chopped into ribbons
1	teaspoon sea salt
½	teaspoon ground black pepper
1	cup mashed leftover Miso-Roasted Kabocha Squash, skin removed
24	large dried pasta shells (about 7 oz/213 g total weight)
½	cup shredded vegan Parmesan

MAKES 4 TO 6 SERVINGS There's something very satisfying about stuffing jumbo pasta shells. I don't know how to describe it, but this dinner is a pleasure to put together! I've mixed leftover Miso-Roasted Kabocha Squash with a tangy tofu ricotta mixture. For the sauce you could easily sub in a jar of your favorite store-bought (or homemade) marinara, but I strongly recommend getting a jar of roasted red peppers and making my sauce. Also recommended: Reserve the small amount of roasted red peppers you need for the **Smoky Cheese Spread (page 174)** and make that recipe in the next couple of weeks. Or, if you made that first and have a lonely jar of leftover peppers sitting in the fridge, this is how you'll use 'em up!

Preheat the oven to 425°F.

To make the tofu ricotta, pat the tofu dry with a clean tea towel. Use your hands to crumble the tofu into small pieces in a large mixing bowl. Add the nutritional yeast, garlic, olive oil, lemon juice, basil, sea salt, black pepper, and mashed squash, and mix to combine well.

Bring a large pot of salted water to a boil. Cook the pasta until very al dente, only 7 to 8 minutes. Drain the pasta and rinse under cold water to stop the cooking and allow you to handle the shells.

To make the sauce, add the roasted red peppers, nondairy milk, garlic, tomato paste, olive oil, sea salt, black pepper, and chili flakes to a high-powered blender and blend until very smooth.

ROASTED RED PEPPER SAUCE (MAKES ABOUT 2 CUPS)

1	jar (12 oz/340 g) roasted red peppers, drained (about 3 whole peppers)
1	cup unsweetened nondairy milk
3	large garlic cloves
2	tablespoons tomato paste
1	tablespoon extra-virgin olive oil
½	teaspoon sea salt
½	teaspoon ground black pepper
¼	teaspoon chili flakes (optional)

Pour the sauce into a saucepan over medium heat and bring to a low simmer. Stir constantly and simmer for 10 to 15 minutes, until reduced by half and slightly thicker. Lower the heat if necessary to prevent splatters or boiling over. In a baking dish that's either 9 by 9 inches or 8 by 10 inches, pour half of the roasted red pepper sauce into the bottom and spread out into an even layer.

Using a heaping cookie scoop, or about 2 tablespoons, fill each pasta shell with the tofu ricotta mixture and place the shells in the baking dish on an angle, rather than flat down, so you can fit them. Top with the remaining roasted red pepper sauce and the shredded vegan Parmesan.

Bake uncovered for 20 minutes. Then broil for 5 minutes to get the top golden brown and crispy.

You can also assemble the whole dish a day ahead, cover with foil, and bake covered for the same amount of time, broiling at the end to get the top crispy.

Continued

MISO-ROASTED KABOCHA SQUASH 3 WAYS

Continued

use leftover Miso-Roasted Kabocha Squash (page 95)

KABOCHA FILLING

1	cup mashed leftover Miso-Roasted Kabocha Squash, skin removed
½	cup shredded vegan Parmesan
1	tablespoon finely chopped fresh sage
1	tablespoon nutritional yeast
	Sea salt and ground black pepper, to taste

RAVIOLI

28	round vegan wonton wrappers

MISO BUTTER SAUCE

3	tablespoons vegan butter, softened to room temperature
1	tablespoon mellow white miso
1	tablespoon minced garlic (2 to 3 large cloves)
¼	cup whole sage leaves
⅓	cup walnuts, coarsely chopped
	Ground black pepper, to taste

KABOCHA WONTON RAVIOLI WITH MISO BUTTER

 30 mins. 10 mins.

MAKES 14 RAVIOLI (2 SERVINGS) If you have some leftover kabocha squash and wonton wrappers ready to go—maybe left over from the **Roasted Vegetable Potstickers (page 78)**—make this gratifying and comforting ravioli with a miso butter sage sauce. Yes, miso butter. Your life from this moment forward is entirely altered. Miso butter is also great on sourdough toast, tossed with spaghetti, or sautéed with veggies. I'd even smother tofu with it and bake or fry it! If you want to save some time on the day you plan to serve this, you can make the filling and miso butter sauce and assemble the ravioli ahead of time.

To make the filling, in a bowl, combine the mashed squash, shredded vegan Parmesan, sage, nutritional yeast, sea salt, and black pepper and set aside.

To make the ravioli, have a small bowl of water near you and a large baking sheet lined with a Silpat mat or parchment paper. Lay out 14 wonton wrappers on the baking sheet. Dollop a heaping tablespoon of filling in the center of each. One at a time, wet the edges of the wrapper, place another wrapper on top, and gently press the filling a little. Using your fingertips, start pressing the two edges together all the way around as you also press around the filling to get rid of any air gaps. Use a small dab of water around both edges again to help them stick together.

You can place a tea towel over this baking sheet and refrigerate until ready to cook the ravioli, or you can freeze the whole tray without the tea towel. Once the ravioli are frozen solid, you can place them in a freezer-safe container or bag.

To make the miso butter sauce, in a small dish combine the softened vegan butter, miso, and garlic. Mix until smooth and well combined and set aside.

Heat a large dry cast-iron pan or nonstick pan over medium heat and toast the walnuts for 3 to 5 minutes, until fragrant and golden brown, tossing occasionally and keeping a close eye on them so they don't burn. Transfer to a dish and set aside for garnishing. Let the pan cool off.

Meanwhile, bring a large pot of salted water to a boil. Set one ravioli in the boiling water at a time using a slotted spoon. This will help

prevent them from sticking. Boil 2 or 3 batches at a time for about 2 minutes, or until they start to float. If boiling from frozen, it will take 3 to 4 minutes. Remove one at a time with a slotted spoon and place on a plate. Reserve about ⅔ cup of the pasta water. It's fine if you take the water from the pot before all the ravioli is finished, as long as half of them have boiled in it.

If you can multitask, cook the ravioli and the sauce at the same time. Heat the pan you used for the walnuts over medium-low heat, add the miso butter mixture, and whisk while it melts. Add the sage leaves and fry for about 2 minutes. If the pan starts getting too hot, turn the heat to low. You shouldn't see any smoke! Add ⅓ cup of the pasta water and whisk vigorously and constantly to combine the sauce, cooking over a low simmer for 3 minutes or so, until slightly reduced and a shade darker in color. Add more pasta water as needed to keep the sauce smooth. Either pour the sauce over the just-boiled ravioli or, if you need to warm up the ravioli, add them to the pan with the sauce over low heat for 1 to 2 minutes, tossing each ravioli only once.

Garnish with the toasted walnuts and black pepper, to taste.

Continued

MISO-ROASTED KABOCHA SQUASH 3 WAYS

Continued

use leftover Miso-Roasted Kabocha Squash (page 95)

INGREDIENTS

1   tablespoon vegan chicken-flavored bouillon base or 2 cubes

3   cups water

1   cup coarsely chopped leftover Miso-Roasted Kabocha Squash, skin removed

½   cup canned full-fat coconut milk

1   tablespoon peeled and coarsely chopped ginger

¼   teaspoon Chinese five spice powder

1   teaspoon neutral vegetable oil

3   baby bok choy heads, cut in half lengthwise

2   cups shiitake mushrooms, stems removed (8 to 10 mushrooms)

½   cup fresh or frozen corn kernels
      Sea salt and ground black pepper, to taste

1   package (14 oz/400 g) fresh udon
      Black sesame seeds, for garnish
      Chiu chow chili oil, to taste (optional)

KABOCHA BROTH WITH UDON

 15 mins.   25 mins.

MAKES 2 SERVINGS This broth is utterly delicious, and you can make it without the coconut milk if you'd rather. But this could also be a good opportunity to use the remaining coconut milk/water you've got from a can you've used previously! I love fresh thick udon noodles as opposed to the dried type, but use what you can find. If you want to forgo the noodles, the **Roasted Vegetable Potstickers (page 78)** would be a great thing to plunk into this broth with other veggies you've got around. And really, all of what I've included in the final soup is entirely optional. It would go great with sautéed broccoli, cabbage, snow peas, and onion. Throw some fried tofu in there too, and you have a complete, cozy meal.

In a high-powered blender, add the bouillon and water (or substitute 3 cups vegetable stock), as well as the squash, coconut milk, ginger, and five spice powder and blend until very smooth. Transfer to a pot.

Heat up a cast-iron grill pan over medium-high heat. Brush with the oil and add the bok choy, cut-side-down. Cook for 2 to 3 minutes on each side. Remove and set aside. Grill the shiitakes for 3 to 4 minutes on each side. As the mushrooms cook down and shrink, making more room in the pan, add the corn and get a light char on the kernels, grilling about 2 minutes. Transfer the mushrooms and corn to a plate. Season with sea salt and black pepper.

Meanwhile, heat the broth over high heat. Once it's at a low boil, add the udon and cook for about 3 minutes or according to the package. Do not overcook the noodles or let them sit in the broth too long or they will get soggy. If only eating one portion, heat the broth to a boil and cook the noodles separately. If using dried udon, you'll want to cook the noodles in a separate pot of water, as they'll take longer. Add sea salt, to taste, to the broth if using vegetable stock.

Pour the noodles and broth in a bowl and top with the grilled vegetables. Serve garnished with black sesame seeds and chili oil.

CAULIFLOWER STEAKS 2 WAYS, WITH SPAGHETTI AGLIO E OLIO (PICCATA & PARM)

⬦ 15 mins. ♨ 50 mins.

CAULIFLOWER PICCATA

2	large heads cauliflower
3	tablespoons olive oil or avocado oil
½	teaspoon sea salt
2	tablespoons vegan butter
¼	cup minced shallot (about 1 shallot)
2	tablespoons minced garlic (3 to 4 large cloves)
1	teaspoon gluten-free all-purpose flour or all-purpose flour
½	cup hot water
½	teaspoon vegan chicken-flavored bouillon base or half a cube
¼	cup capers + 1 tablespoon caper brine
2	tablespoons lemon juice (about 1 lemon)
2	tablespoons unsweetened nondairy milk
¼	teaspoon ground black pepper
⅓	cup finely chopped fresh parsley, divided

MAKES 4 SERVINGS (OF EACH OPTION) I am the cauli queen and wanted to give ya this idea for cauliflower two ways, served with spaghetti aglio e olio. You need more of this cruciferous veg in your life, and I'm sure you've been looking for ways to level it up. Piccata and parm are my weapons of choice here, and both are equally mouthwatering and delightful. You can easily halve either option and make only two steaks and half the sauce for less leftovers, and you can use the cauliflower florets that remain from cutting the steaks to build up to the quantity needed for the **Korean BBQ Burritos (page 140)**.

Preheat the oven to 450°F. Line a baking sheet with parchment paper.

To prepare the cauliflower for both recipes, remove the leafy parts, being careful not to cut off any florets. Slice each head in half from the top. From the inside of each half, cut a slice ¾ to 1 inch thick, creating 4 cross-sections or steaks. Place them on the baking sheet, brush with an even layer of oil on both sides and the edges, and sprinkle with sea salt. Roast for 35 to 40 minutes, flipping halfway through, until golden brown and fork-tender.

To make the cauliflower piccata, while the steaks are roasting, in a large cast-iron pan over medium-low heat, melt the vegan butter. Add the shallots and sauté for 1 to 2 minutes, until soft. Add the garlic and sauté for 1 more minute, until fragrant. Add the flour, whisking constantly until mixed in, and cook another 2 to 3 minutes. Add the hot water, bouillon, capers, caper brine, lemon juice, and nondairy milk. Stir until combined, and cook another 2 to 3 minutes, stirring constantly, until you can draw a line in the sauce with the back of a spoon. Stir in the black pepper and half the parsley, then remove from the heat until the cauliflower is done roasting.

Continued

CAULIFLOWER STEAKS 2 WAYS, WITH SPAGHETTI AGLIO E OLIO (PICCATA & PARM)

Continued

CAULIFLOWER PARM

2	large heads cauliflower
3	tablespoons olive oil or avocado oil
½	teaspoon sea salt
¼	cup Italian-style bread crumbs
1	tablespoon nutritional yeast
1	cup store-bought marinara sauce
4	slices vegan mozzarella or provolone cheese
4	fresh basil leaves
	Ground black pepper, for garnish

SPAGHETTI AGLIO E OLIO

⅔	package (1 lb/454 g) spaghetti
¼	cup extra-virgin olive oil
2	tablespoons minced garlic (3 or 4 large cloves)
1	teaspoon chili flakes
½	teaspoon sea salt
½	teaspoon ground black pepper
¾	cup shredded vegan Parmesan, divided
¼	cup finely chopped fresh parsley

To make the cauliflower parm, while the steaks are roasting (see page 136), combine the bread crumbs with the nutritional yeast and set aside. After roasting the cauliflower, add ¼ cup marinara, a slice of vegan cheese, and a basil leaf to each steak and then generously cover the entire top in the bread crumb mixture. Move your rack to the top third of the oven under the broiler and broil for 5 to 7 minutes, until the cheese is melted and the bread crumbs are golden brown.

To make the spaghetti aglio e olio, while the steaks are roasting, bring a large pot of salted water to a boil and cook the spaghetti until al dente. Reserve ½ cup of the pasta cooking water before draining and set aside. Drain the pasta but do not rinse.

Place the same pot immediately back over low heat and add the olive oil, garlic, chili flakes, sea salt, and black pepper. Cook for 1 to 2 minutes, until the garlic is softer and fragrant. Add the drained spaghetti, ¼ cup of the reserved pasta water, ½ cup of the shredded vegan Parmesan, and the parsley and cook another minute, tossing to coat evenly.

If the cauliflower piccata sauce has become too thick while being set aside, spoon a couple tablespoons at a time of the remaining reserved pasta water into the sauce to thin it out, and reheat if necessary before serving.

Portion the spaghetti aglio e olio onto plates. For the piccata, place a roasted cauliflower steak next to it and spoon the piccata sauce over top. Garnish with remaining vegan Parmesan and remaining parsley. For the parm, place a broiled steak next to the spaghetti and garnish with remaining vegan Parmesan and ground black pepper.

KOREAN BBQ BURRITOS

 25 mins. 35 mins.

 10 mins. soaking

use Gochujang Aioli (page 191)

leftover cauliflower florets from making Cauliflower Steaks 2 Ways (page 136)

BURRITOS

2	cups dried soy curls or vegan chicken pieces
2	tablespoons brown sugar or coconut sugar
2	tablespoons toasted sesame oil
2	tablespoons gluten-free tamari or low-sodium soy sauce
2	teaspoons gochujang (use more for hot)
1	teaspoon chipotle chili powder
1	teaspoon granulated garlic powder
1	teaspoon vegan beef-flavored bouillon base or 1 cube, or vegan Worcestershire
½	teaspoon ground ginger
½	teaspoon sea salt
1	green bell pepper, thinly sliced
1	white or yellow onion, thinly sliced

ROASTED CAULIFLOWER RICE (MAKES ABOUT 1⅔ CUPS)

5–6	cups cauliflower florets
¼	cup packed fresh cilantro, finely chopped
¼	cup finely minced green onion (white and light green parts)
½	teaspoon ground cumin
1	tablespoon avocado oil or neutral vegetable oil

MAKES 4 BURRITOS The soy curls are back in action, but this time they're soaking up some Korean BBQ flaves! If you haven't brought gochujang (Korean chili pepper paste) into your condiment selection, you've been missing out. If Sriracha is a college kid's condiment, gochujang is a thirty-something's hot sauce of choice. It's more nuanced and sophisticated in its flavors. Since I also wanted to use up the leftover cauliflower florets from the cauliflower steaks recipe, I stuffed an herby cauliflower rice into these burritos. It's nice and light, which you'll need 'cause the soy curls are filling and regular rice would be overboard.

Preheat the oven to 425°F.

Line 2 large baking sheets with parchment paper. You can use a Silpat mat for one of the sheets, which you'll put the soy curls on. I wouldn't recommend using Silpat for the other one, which is for the cauliflower rice, pepper, and onion, as it will steam rather than roast.

To make the burritos, add the soy curls to a bowl and pour water over them until covered. Soak for about 10 minutes, until expanded. If using vegan chicken pieces, you can skip this step.

Meanwhile, in another mixing bowl, combine the sugar, sesame oil, tamari or soy sauce, gochujang, chili powder, garlic powder, bouillon base, ginger, and sea salt. Before draining the soy curls, reserve 2 tablespoons of the soaking water and add to the sauce mixture. If using vegan chicken, add 2 tablespoons fresh water. Squeeze the moisture out of the soy curls through a sieve using your hands. Add the soy curls to the sauce and toss until well coated.

Spread out the soy curls on the Silpat- or parchment-lined baking sheet.

To make the cauliflower rice, to a food processor add the florets in 2 or 3 batches. Pulse them into small pieces until they resemble rice. You should have 3½ to 4 cups of raw cauliflower rice. Transfer to a bowl and add the cilantro, green onion, cumin, and oil. Mix until well combined.

Add the cauliflower rice to one half of the other large baking sheet lined with parchment. Add the green pepper and onion to the other half.

ASSEMBLY

4	large (10-inch) flour tortillas
1	batch Gochujang Aioli
1	cup vegan mozzarella or Cheddar shreds
1	cup thinly sliced napa cabbage
½	cup store-bought vegan kimchi
2	tablespoons sesame seeds

Place both baking sheets in the oven and bake for 20 minutes, flipping the soy curls, onion, and pepper halfway through. Soy curls should take 18 to 20 minutes total. The green pepper and onion need an additional 5 to 8 minutes to get slightly browned and cooked through. Transfer the green pepper and onion to the sheet that you set aside with the baked soy curls.

Spread the cauliflower rice across the whole baking sheet to finish baking. Bake for 5 to 8 minutes longer, until some of the cauliflower rice gets brown and crispy.

To assemble the burritos, place a tortilla on a work surface. You might need to microwave each tortilla for 10 seconds just before assembling to get it slightly warm for folding more easily. Spread a spoonful of gochujang aioli in the center of the tortilla. For each burrito, add a quarter of the soy curls, cauliflower rice, vegan cheese, napa cabbage, and roasted onion and green pepper; 2 tablespoons of kimchi; and ½ tablespoon of sesame seeds. Drizzle more gochujang aioli on top and roll it up tightly. Slice in half to serve. Repeat with the remaining burritos.

BUFFALO CHICKEN CRUNCH WRAPS

20 mins.   44 mins.

C   10 mins. soaking

use Jalapeño Ranch (page 190)

BUFFALO SOY CURLS

2	cups dried soy curls
½	cup buffalo-style hot sauce
3	tablespoons melted vegan butter
2	tablespoons apple cider vinegar
2	tablespoons finely chopped chives
1	tablespoon finely chopped fresh dill
2	teaspoons vegan chicken-flavored bouillon base or 1 cube
1	teaspoon onion powder
1	teaspoon granulated garlic powder
½	teaspoon chipotle chili powder
½	teaspoon sea salt
½	teaspoon ground black pepper

CRUNCH WRAPS

8	large (10-inch) flour tortillas
4	(5- to 6-inch) flat corn tostada shells
2	cups vegan pepper Jack or mozzarella shreds
¼	cup finely diced carrot (1 small carrot)
¼	cup finely diced celery (1 small stalk)
1	batch Jalapeño Ranch
1	cup finely chopped romaine lettuce
1¼	tablespoons neutral vegetable oil, divided

MAKES 4 WRAPS You aren't sick of buffalo stuff yet, right? I would hope not! This is the same recipe for buffalo chicken soy curls from the **Buffalo Chicken Mac n' Cheese (page 113)**, but with double the amount of soy curls and using all the sauce to coat them. They're going to bring the heat while you crunch down on cool deliciousness. Layered in these babies is Jalapeño Ranch, romaine lettuce, celery, and carrots. The vegan pepper Jack cheese is the glue that holds it all together, but what makes it a crunch wrap is the crunchy tostada in the middle—otherwise this would basically be a quesadilla. You could easily put the Buffalo Mac n' Cheese in this same little setup, too, if yer real crazy!

Preheat the oven to 425°F. Line a baking sheet with a Silpat mat or parchment paper.

To make the buffalo soy curls, put the soy curls in a bowl and pour water over top until covered. Let the soy curls hydrate and expand for about 10 minutes. Before draining the soy curls, reserve 2 teaspoons of the soaking liquid. Drain the soy curls in a fine-mesh sieve, squeezing out excess water with your hands, and set aside.

In the same bowl, combine the hot sauce, melted vegan butter, apple cider vinegar, chives, dill, bouillon base, reserved soaking liquid, onion powder, garlic powder, chili powder, sea salt, and black pepper. Add the drained soy curls and toss to coat evenly in the sauce.

Transfer the soy curls to the prepared baking sheet. Bake for 18 to 20 minutes, flipping halfway through, until golden and browned in spots.

To build the crunch wraps, stack 4 large tortillas and place a tostada shell in the center. Using a paring knife, trace around the edge of the tostada to cut 4 smaller tortilla rounds. You can use the excess scraps of flour tortillas to make the tortilla strips for **Tortilla Soup (page 46)**.

Add the cheese shreds to the center of each remaining large tortilla, filling a round space as large as the tostada, which will go in the center. Add a quarter of the buffalo soy curls, carrots, and celery, then drizzle with the jalapeño ranch and place a tostada shell on top. Add a bit more cheese and the romaine lettuce and

place the smaller tortilla cutout on top. Tightly fold the edges of the large tortilla toward the center, creating pleats. Quickly invert the crunch wraps so the pleats are on the bottom and they stay together.

Once all the crunch wraps are assembled, heat a nonstick pan over medium-low heat with a teaspoon of oil coating the bottom. Fry one crunch wrap at a time, placing the pleat side down in the center of the pan and cooking for 3 minutes per side until golden brown. Lower the heat if necessary as you fry the remaining crunch wraps. Let the crunch wrap rest a few minutes before cutting in half. Use

SLOPPY JOE ZUCCHINI BOATS

25 mins.   70 mins.

INGREDIENTS

4	large zucchini
3	tablespoons olive oil, divided
1	cup finely chopped white or yellow onion (about 1 onion)
1	cup finely diced green bell pepper (about 1 pepper)
2	tablespoons coconut sugar or light brown sugar
2	tablespoons gluten-free tamari or low-sodium soy sauce
1	tablespoon minced garlic (about 2 large cloves)
2	teaspoons vegan beef-flavored bouillon base or 2 cubes
2	teaspoons chili powder
2	teaspoons onion powder
1	teaspoon smoked paprika
1	teaspoon sea salt
1	teaspoon ground black pepper
1	package (13.7 oz/390 g) veggie ground round (about 3 cups)
2	cups canned crushed fire-roasted tomatoes
¼	cup vegan Worcestershire
2	cups mixed vegan cheese shreds (1 cup each mozzarella and Cheddar)
3	tablespoons Italian-style bread crumbs

MAKES 8 BOATS Sure, you can make this sloppy joe filling and eat it on a soft kaiser, but that's so basic. I want to give you a healthier option so you can eat even more sloppy joe stuff. You can round out these zucchini boats with garlic bread or rice on the side and serve as a meal. Or, if you're too lazy to prep the zucchini altogether, just pour the sloppy joe mixture into an oven-safe dish, top with the vegan cheese shreds, and bake for 20 minutes until melty! Serve with slices of garlic toast for dipping, a perfect last-minute party appie.

Cut each zucchini in half lengthwise. Use a paring knife to score around the inside edge about ¼ inch from the sides, being careful not to cut through the zucchini. Use a spoon to carefully scoop out the flesh. You'll have about 4 cups of zucchini flesh scraped out, which you can use for the **Zucchini Carbonara (page 146)**.

Take 1 tablespoon of the oil and brush both sides of the zucchini boats with a light layer. Arrange the zucchini halves side-by-side on a large baking sheet with the hollowed parts facing up.

In a large nonstick pan, heat the remaining 2 tablespoons oil over medium heat. Add the onion and green pepper and sauté for 3 minutes. Add the coconut sugar, tamari, garlic, bouillon base, chili powder, onion powder, smoked paprika, sea salt, and black pepper, and cook for another 2 minutes. Add the ground round, crushed tomatoes, and Worcestershire, stir to combine, and cook for another 5 to 6 minutes. Cover the pan, lower the heat to medium-low, and cook for 20 minutes, until reduced, thick, and darker brown.

Preheat the oven to 425°F.

Spoon the sloppy joe mixture generously into the zucchini boats, piling the mixture above the edges. Top with the vegan cheese shreds and sprinkle the bread crumbs evenly on top of each. Bake for 35 minutes, until the zucchini is tender and the cheese is melted. Broil for 3 to 5 minutes to crisp up the top, if necessary.

ZUCCHINI CARBONARA

 10 mins. 25 mins.

*use leftover zucchini
from making Sloppy Joe
Zucchini Boats (page 145)*

*Tempeh Bacon Chunks
(page 100; optional)*

INGREDIENTS

1	tablespoon olive oil
4	cups peeled and coarsely chopped zucchini
¼	cup coarsely chopped garlic (5 or 6 large garlic cloves)
¼	cup garlic dill pickle brine or sauerkraut brine
2	tablespoons vegan butter
2	tablespoons nutritional yeast
1	teaspoon ground black pepper, plus more for garnish
1	package (1 lb/454 g) spaghetti
2	cups finely chopped or crumbled Tempeh Bacon Chunks, vegan bacon, or smoky sausage
1	teaspoon kala namak
½	cup shredded vegan Parmesan, for garnish

MAKES 4 TO 6 SERVINGS This is one of my most popular *RECIPE?!* creations from the YouTube channel. I've lost count of how many times I've received notifications of y'all making this on social media…so thank you! Well, I too love this recipe and make it all the time. It was inspired by my trip to Italy a few years ago. A couple of the vegan restaurants I ate at were using zucchini to make a cream sauce, and I was like, *DUH,* why didn't I think of that! It works well as a carbonara because it's a neutral base and not too thick, unlike cashews or tofu. If you don't have zucchini flesh left from making the Sloppy Joe Zucchini Boats, you can make this from scratch by peeling a couple of whole zucchini, coarsely chopping the flesh, and measuring out 4 cups. If you don't want to use Tempeh Bacon Chunks, you can crumble and brown up any other vegan bacon or smoky sausage product you like instead. If making the tempeh bacon chunks from scratch for this recipe, get the tempeh in the marinade and set aside while you cook the zucchini and garlic for the sauce. I recommend making the pieces of tempeh bacon small like a crumble for this recipe, and rather than baking it, you will pan-fry the tempeh. Just in case you don't know what brine is, it's the liquid from a jar of pickles or sauerkraut, and it's the other key ingredient in this recipe. The kala namak is also important for its eggy flavor, since we're not incorporating eggs into this sauce like a traditional carbonara.

Heat a large cast-iron or nonstick pan over medium heat and add the olive oil. Once the oil is hot, add the zucchini and garlic and sauté for 9 to 10 minutes, stirring occasionally, until the zucchini is soft and cooked. There should still be a small amount of water from the zucchini bubbling on the bottom of the pan. Add the zucchini to a blender along with the pickle brine, vegan butter, nutritional yeast, and black pepper and blend on high until very smooth.

Meanwhile, bring a large pot of salted water to a boil and cook the spaghetti until al dente.

If making the tempeh bacon from scratch, heat the same pan over medium heat and once the pan is hot, add the marinated tempeh bacon in an even layer. Cook on the first side, allowing it to brown and caramelize, for 5 to 6 minutes. Toss and flip the pieces, cooking for another 5 minutes and lowering the heat if it starts to burn or

get too hot. If using a premade bacon or sausage product, brown it in the pan with a bit of oil until cooked.

Transfer the tempeh bacon, vegan bacon, or sausage to another dish. Place the pan back over low heat, add the zucchini cream sauce, and simmer for 2 minutes. Turn off the heat and whisk in the kala namak right before you add the pasta. By this point, your pasta should be cooked to al dente, so you can add it right from the boiling water into the pan of sauce with a pair of tongs or drain it and then add to the sauce. Add the tempeh bacon or browned bacon or sausage and toss until combined.

Garnish each serving with shredded vegan Parmesan and more black pepper.

If reheating leftovers, you'll want to add a bit of water or nondairy milk and a bit of vegan butter to the pan to get the sauce loose and smooth again.

stuff I eat...when I'm busy

Busy is just an excuse, but there are some days where it feels like the clock is on fast forward and I could skip eating all together! I know: me, skip a meal? It happens, but if I'm just a little prepared a few days prior, then I've got food in the fridge and usually SOMETHING to heat up real quick. This is usually what this day looks like on paper...overwhelmed breakdown not included!

BREAKFAST

my fave smoothie (page 43)

Prep advice: Always have frozen bananas in the freezer! If you're a real go-getter, you can even put everything for the smoothie, minus the liquid, in serving jars in the freezer for each day of the week. Dump the contents in the blender, add the nondairy milk and coffee, blend, and serve in the same jar.

LUNCH

reheated leftover pasta dish
pictured is the zucchini carbonara
(page 146)

Prep advice: Cook the noodles and make tempeh bacon chunks and the sauce for the pasta at the start of the week, then it's as easy as heat-and-serve if you don't have leftovers already.

DINNER

my everyday roasted vegetable
salad (page 76)

Prep advice: Try roasting the vegetables at the start of the week or for a Sunday dinner and make the dressing (maybe a double batch) as well. Leftover roasted vegetables can be nuked for a salad. When preparing kale for a salad, I usually chop up enough for two or three servings and reserve the rest in a container in the fridge. Only massage and dress what you'll eat for one salad at a time.

CRISPY TOFU FINGERS 2 WAYS

I'm about to take the Crispy Tofu Fingers from the Bowl Bible to new and ambitious heights, because a vegan can never tire of tofu . . . at least if I'm in charge. These crunchy and chewy morsels are about to level up a divine salad and hit just right in a comforting dinner idea that'll soon be famous at your table. I look forward to seeing more unique ways y'all use them too!

CHARRED CORN SALAD

 20 mins.   12 mins.

use Crispy Tofu Fingers (page 92)

Jalapeño Ranch (page 190)

INGREDIENTS

1	teaspoon olive oil
3½	cups fresh or frozen corn kernels
1	batch Jalapeño Ranch
1	teaspoon chipotle chili powder (optional)
3	cups packed arugula
1	cup packed shredded red cabbage
1	jalapeño, thinly sliced
4	cocktail tomatoes, cut into wedges
½	cup thinly sliced red onion (about half an onion)
1	avocado, thinly sliced
2	tablespoons coarsely chopped fresh mint
2	tablespoons coarsely chopped fresh dill
1	batch Crispy Tofu Fingers

MAKES 4 SERVINGS It's essentially a salad of all the veg I don't mind eating raw. The fresh mint and dill make it pop, while the creamy richness of Jalapeño Ranch and the warm charred corn make it kinda cozy. Then throw the crispy tofu on top and you've got yourself a comfort-foodie kind of salad. For an even quicker version, skip the crispy tofu and use store-bought breaded vegan chicken fingers and slice them up on top! I do this often.

In a large cast-iron pan over high heat, add the olive oil and corn in an even layer. Cook for 5 to 6 minutes without tossing. Then only toss occasionally so the corn gets charred and caramelized, about another 6 minutes. Remove the pan from the heat.

Mix the jalapeño ranch with the chipotle chili powder.

Build the salad on a platter or in a large bowl by layering the arugula, cabbage, jalapeño slices, tomato wedges, sliced onion, sliced avocado, mint, and dill and then piling the corn on top. Add the tofu fingers and drizzle with jalapeño ranch mixture.

Continued

CRISPY TOFU FINGERS 2 WAYS

Continued

use Crispy Tofu Fingers (page 92)

Pumpkin Miso Gravy (page 193)

CREAMY MASHED POTATOES

5–6	cups peeled and cubed white or yellow potato, 1-inch cubes (about 5 potatoes)
¼	cup vegan butter
½	teaspoon sea salt
½	teaspoon ground black pepper
¼	cup finely chopped chives

TOPPINGS

2	cups fresh or frozen corn
2	cups fresh or frozen green beans
1	batch Pumpkin Miso Gravy
1	batch Crispy Tofu Fingers

HFF FAMOUS BOWLS

 20 mins.   20 mins.

MAKES 4 SERVINGS Technically this bowl isn't famous yet because this is the first time you're seeing it. But it's obviously an ode to the KFC Famous Bowl and it will become famous in no time, I'm sure! The Crispy Tofu Fingers can do no wrong when paired with creamy, silky mashed potatoes and the epic Pumpkin Miso Gravy. I actually made the gravy first when I was testing recipes for this cookbook, and it reminded me so much of chicken gravy that I was inspired to use it in this comforting concoction!

To make the mashed potatoes, add the potato cubes to a large pot of cold water. Bring the pot to a boil, about 10 minutes. Placing a lid on the pot slightly off to the side to let heat escape will speed up the process. Cook for 13 to 15 minutes, until a potato easily slides off a fork. Drain the potatoes in a colander.

If you want the creamiest mashed potatoes, I love using a ricer. Feed the cooked potato chunks through the smallest holes of the ricer into the pot and fold together with the vegan butter, sea salt, black pepper, and chives until combined. Otherwise, add the cooked potatoes back into the pot with the vegan butter, sea salt, and black pepper and mash by hand with a potato masher until mostly smooth. Fold in the chives until combined.

To make the toppings, in a pot with a steamer insert, steam the corn and green beans together until cooked through and tender, 3 to 5 minutes. The green beans should still appear bright green and slightly crisp.

Meanwhile, if reheating from leftovers or if made in advance, in a saucepan over medium-low heat or in the microwave, heat the pumpkin miso gravy adding a small amount of stock or water to thin it out, if necessary.

To assemble, scoop the mashed potatoes into a serving bowl. Top with the steamed vegetables, fresh-baked crispy tofu fingers, and a generous amount of pumpkin miso gravy.

MUSHROOM KRAUT POTATO CAKES

 25 mins. 22 mins.

use leftover mashed potatoes from HFF Famous Bowls (page 153)

MAKES 8 CAKES I know what you're thinking…leftover mashed potatoes?! No such thing! But if you're cooking for one, which I am most of the time, there are leftovers! Either way, you can easily make mashed potatoes to turn them into these luscious potato cakes if you definitely won't EVER have leftovers of them in your fridge. Any excuse for more mashed potatoes, am I right? The combo of mushrooms and sauerkraut that I stuff into these cakes gives them a nice savory bite, but you could experiment with other fillings like veggie ground round or sausage, maybe the **Tempeh Bacon Chunks (page 100)**, or the **Sloppy Joe filling (page 145)**. If you have any of that stuff left over, let your imagination carry you away!

INGREDIENTS

2	cups leftover mashed potatoes
2	tablespoons gluten-free all-purpose flour or all-purpose flour
¼	teaspoon smoked paprika
1¼	tablespoons avocado oil or neutral vegetable oil, divided
½	cup finely chopped cremini mushrooms (6 to 8 mushrooms)
¼	cup finely chopped white onion (about half a small onion)
2	teaspoons minced garlic (1 or 2 large cloves)
¼	cup sauerkraut, drained of excess liquid
1	tablespoon finely chopped fresh dill, plus more for garnish
	Sea salt and ground black pepper, to taste
1	cup vegan sour cream, for serving

Mix the leftover mashed potatoes with the flour and smoked paprika and set aside.

In a nonstick pan, heat ¼ tablespoon of the oil over medium heat. Sauté the mushrooms, onion, and garlic for about 5 minutes, until slightly caramelized and the water is evaporated from the mushrooms. Add to a bowl with the sauerkraut, dill, sea salt, and black pepper. Wipe out the pan, as you will use it to fry the potato cakes.

To assemble the potato cakes, portion out ¼ cup of mashed potatoes into your hands and roll into a ball. Cut the ball in half; the two halves are the top and bottom of the potato cake. Gently flatten one half while holding it in your palm, then portion 1 tablespoon of filling into the center. Place the other half on top, slightly flatten it, then pinch the edges together around the circumference of the potato cake. Pat your hands gently around the edges and top to pack the cake and gently flatten it to about 3 inches wide. Place the assembled potato cakes on a cutting board or baking sheet.

Once all the potato cakes are assembled, heat the pan over medium heat with the remaining 1 tablespoon oil. Once the oil is hot, add 4 cakes at a time to the pan, spaced apart, and fry for 3 to 4 minutes on each side, until golden brown. Transfer the cooked potato cakes to a wire rack. Serve with the vegan sour cream.

HOT TIP If you have leftover **Pumpkin Miso Gravy (page 193)**, it works well here as a swap for the sour cream.

snacks,
staples &
saucy stuff

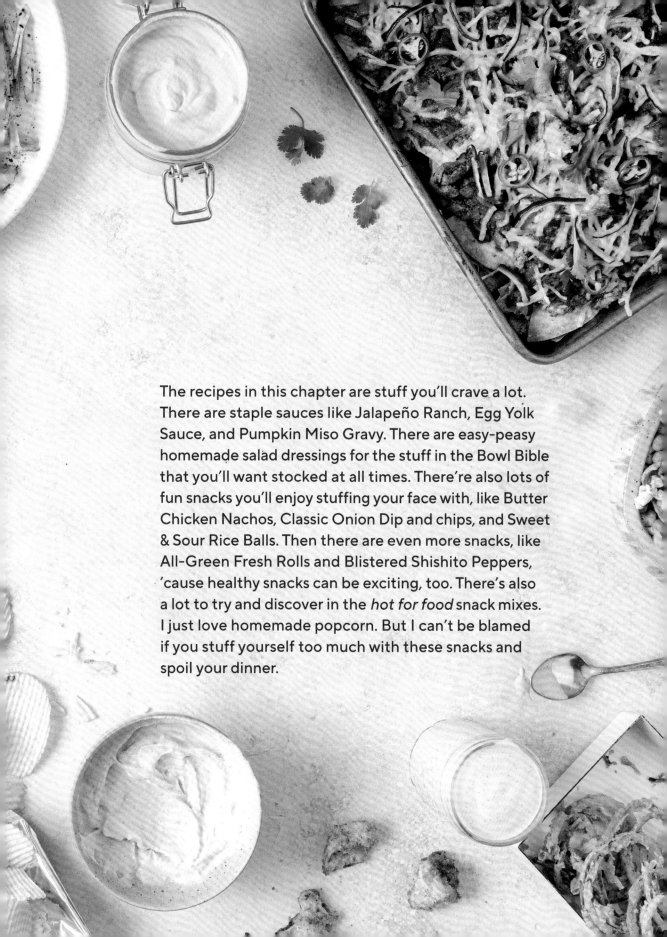

The recipes in this chapter are stuff you'll crave a lot. There are staple sauces like Jalapeño Ranch, Egg Yolk Sauce, and Pumpkin Miso Gravy. There are easy-peasy homemade salad dressings for the stuff in the Bowl Bible that you'll want stocked at all times. There're also lots of fun snacks you'll enjoy stuffing your face with, like Butter Chicken Nachos, Classic Onion Dip and chips, and Sweet & Sour Rice Balls. Then there are even more snacks, like All-Green Fresh Rolls and Blistered Shishito Peppers, 'cause healthy snacks can be exciting, too. There's also a lot to try and discover in the *hot for food* snack mixes. I just love homemade popcorn. But I can't be blamed if you stuff yourself too much with these snacks and spoil your dinner.

HOT TIP If you don't have one or two of the spices listed for the sauce (garam masala, whole mustard seed, cumin, and curry powder), you can still make this. You could also use fenugreek if you have that or use ground mustard instead of the whole seeds. The motto: Make it work!

BUTTER CHICKEN NACHOS

 20 mins. 35 mins.

*use Cilantro Sour Cream
(page 189)*

Chicken Shawarma (page 99)

**BUTTER CHICKEN SAUCE
(MAKES ABOUT 2 CUPS)**

1	tablespoon coconut oil
1	cup very finely chopped white onion (about 1 large onion)
2	tablespoons minced garlic (3 or 4 large cloves)
1	tablespoon peeled and minced fresh ginger
1½	teaspoons garam masala
1	teaspoon whole mustard seed
1	teaspoon ground cumin
1	teaspoon yellow curry powder
1	teaspoon sea salt
½	teaspoon ground turmeric
1	cup canned full-fat coconut milk
½	cup canned crushed fire-roasted tomatoes
2	tablespoons vegan butter
2	cups packed baby spinach

NACHOS

10–11	cups tortilla chips
1	batch Chicken Shawarma (about 2 cups)
1½	cups vegan mozzarella shreds
½	cup thinly sliced red onion
1	jalapeño, thinly sliced
1	batch Cilantro Sour Cream
¼	cup coarsely chopped fresh cilantro, for garnish

MAKES 4 TO 6 SERVINGS You know me, I'm not content with giving you plain ol' anything. It's gotta be leveled up! And that's where these Butter Chicken Nachos come onto the scene. You might recall a video circa 2015, where I made vegan butter chicken on the spot with whatever was in my fridge. It's a classic *RECIPE?!* episode, but that sauce has been a staple ever since. Now ya probably never saw it coming that I'd throw it on top of nachos, but trust me, these are hella good!

Preheat the oven to 425°F. Line a baking sheet with a Silpat mat or parchment paper.

Follow the Chicken Shawarma recipe and bake the soy curls as instructed, or if you have only half a batch of leftover Chicken Shawarma, you could easily halve the butter chicken sauce and make a smaller portion of the nachos.

To make the butter chicken sauce, heat a large nonstick pan over medium heat with the coconut oil. Once the oil is hot, add the onion and sauté for 4 minutes until translucent and slightly browned. Add the garlic, ginger, garam masala, mustard seed, cumin, curry powder, sea salt, and turmeric, stir to combine, and cook for 3 minutes. Add the coconut milk and tomatoes and stir to combine. Reduce the heat to medium-low and cook, stirring occasionally, for 10 to 12 minutes, until the sauce is reduced by about half, thicker, and a dark burnt orange. Turn off the heat. Stir in the vegan butter and spinach. Cover the pan to wilt the spinach, and set aside if your soy curls are still baking.

Once the soy curls are baked, remove from the baking sheet and use the same sheet to assemble the nachos. If using leftover Chicken Shawarma soy curls, you don't need to reheat them.

To assemble the nachos, set the oven to broil. Lay out the chips to fill the baking sheet. Layer with the baked soy curls, spoon the butter chicken sauce all over, and top with mozzarella shreds, red onion, and jalapeños.

Broil for 5 to 7 minutes, until the cheese is melted and the toppings are slightly shrunken. Drizzle the cilantro sour cream on top and garnish with cilantro just before serving.

ALL-GREEN FRESH ROLLS WITH GREEN CURRY DIPPING SAUCE

30 mins. 20–25 mins.

GREEN CURRY DIPPING SAUCE
(MAKES ABOUT ¾ CUP)

½	cup canned coconut cream
¼	cup tightly packed fresh cilantro
2	tablespoons green curry paste
2	large garlic cloves
2	tablespoons lime juice (about 1 lime)
1	tablespoon seasoned rice vinegar
1	teaspoon granulated sugar
¼	teaspoon sea salt
	Pinch chili flakes (optional)

FRESH ROLLS

10	dried rice paper sheets
5	large green leaf lettuce leaves (ribs removed), torn in half
2	avocados, sliced
½	English cucumber, ribboned with a peeler
1½	cups sugar snap peas
1½	cups packed microgreens or sprouts
1½	cups fresh mint leaves
1½	cups fresh basil leaves
1½	cups fresh cilantro leaves

MAKES 10 ROLLS I fell in love with the simplicity of fresh rolls since traveling to Bali. They're on every menu and they all taste amazing! It might just be the tropical heat that makes them taste so good, but I ate my weight in them. It was on my agenda to master making them at home and I decided that filling them with lots of crunchy green stuff would be the game plan. I love that these are all green because, let's face it, most of my best recipes are brown so it's nice to change things up! Even if you can't quite get the hang of rolling them on your first go, it all tastes the same in the end. And just wait until you get that creamy green curry dipping sauce in your mouth. It's fantastic!

To make the green curry sauce, in a high-powered blender, add the coconut cream, cilantro, green curry paste, garlic, lime juice, vinegar, sugar, sea salt, and chili flakes. Blend until very smooth. Transfer to a small saucepan and bring to a low simmer, cooking about 2 to 4 minutes, until slightly thicker and reduced.

Once all your vegetables are prepped for the fresh rolls, fill a wide shallow dish that's slightly larger than the rice paper sheets with tepid water so you can soak the whole sheet. Soak one rice paper sheet at a time, for 10 to 20 seconds. You still want to feel the cross-hatch pattern on the surface of the rice sheets. Don't oversoak or it will be too soft and hard to roll.

Assemble the rolls one at a time. Lay the wet rice paper sheets on a work surface. Add a piece of the lettuce and divide the avocado, cucumber, snap peas, microgreens or sprouts, and fresh herbs among the sheets in whatever order you like. Roll one side of the rice paper over the filling, tucking it in as you start rolling again and also folding the sides in. Continue rolling until completely sealed. Place on a plate or cut in half if you prefer.

Serve with the green curry dipping sauce. Leftover dipping sauce will get thick from refrigeration. Add a teaspoon of water at a time to thin it out until it's a smooth, dippable consistency.

CLASSIC ONION DIP

 15 mins. C 1 hr. refrigeration

INGREDIENTS

1	package (14 oz/397 g) soft tofu
½	cup vegan sour cream
½	cup vegan mayonnaise
1	large shallot, coarsely chopped (about ⅓ cup)
2	tablespoons apple cider vinegar
1	tablespoon lemon juice
1	tablespoon + 1 teaspoon onion powder
2	teaspoons dehydrated minced onion
1	teaspoon vegetable broth powder or 1 onion or vegetable bouillon cube
½	teaspoon sea salt
½	teaspoon ground black pepper
1	bag ridged or ruffled potato chips

MAKES ABOUT 2½ CUPS I take full responsibility for your new addiction to this classic onion dip! It's so killer and extra when it comes to that oniony flavor. It's just like the junky stuff you buy in the tub, but of course, not junky at all. So don't feel too bad about devouring a whole bag of chips with it either. If you want to really level things up, serve this dip with the **Crispy Onion Strings (page 194)**!

Drain the tofu from the package water and place in a nut milk bag or bamboo steamer cloth and squeeze out as much moisture as possible. You should have about 1¼ cups of strained tofu.

To a high-powered blender, add the tofu with the sour cream, mayonnaise, shallot, apple cider vinegar, lemon juice, onion powder, dehydrated onion, vegetable broth powder, sea salt, and black pepper. Blend until very, very smooth. You may need to use the baton to move the mixture closer to the blade while blending or stop the blender and push the mixture off the sides with a spatula a few times in between blending.

Pour into a bowl and refrigerate for at least 1 hour. It's best served after refrigeration, but if you can't wait, it can still be eaten immediately.

HOT TIP If you want to make the **Stuffed Potato Skins (page 164)**, reserve 1 cup of dip before it's all gone!

STUFFED POTATO SKINS WITH ONION DIP

 20 mins. 55 mins.

use leftover Classic Onion Dip (page 163)

INGREDIENTS

4	russet potatoes, well scrubbed
1–2	tablespoons olive oil, divided
	Sea salt and ground black pepper, to taste
1	cup leftover Classic Onion Dip
2	tablespoons finely chopped chives, plus more for garnish
2	tablespoons finely chopped pickled jalapeños
½	teaspoon smoked paprika, plus more for garnish
¾	cup vegan Cheddar shreds

MAKES 8 PIECES If you manage to put some of the Classic Onion Dip aside, you can use it to make these stuffed potato skins—otherwise use this recipe as inspo to make your own version. These are fully loaded (no morsel of potato goes to waste) but if you're looking for just the crispy skins, then when you scoop out the filling, reserve it for another use, like the **Mushroom Kraut Potato Cakes (page 154).** Then you can bake the cheese and other finely chopped toppings right on top of the scraped potato skins and get them nice and crunchy.

Preheat the oven to 450°F.

Cut the potatoes in half lengthwise. Rub all the halves with olive oil on the skin and exposed flesh and sprinkle with sea salt and black pepper. Place flesh-side-up on a baking sheet and bake for 40 minutes until cooked through and soft.

You can let the potatoes cool before you scoop out the filling, but I'm impatient, so I take a small paring knife and cut about ⅛ inch from the edges all around without piercing the skin, then down the length of the center. Use a spoon to scoop out most of the potato. Place the scooped-out potato in a mixing bowl.

Brush the inside of the skins with more olive oil and add sea salt and black pepper to the insides. Broil for 5 to 7 minutes, flipping halfway through.

Mash the scooped-out potato and combine with ¾ cup of the onion dip, the chives, pickled jalapeños, and smoked paprika. Taste it and if you want, add more sea salt.

Brush the inside of the baked skins with a thin layer of the remaining onion dip. Add a sprinkle of the cheese shreds. Scoop the mashed potato mixture into the skins. Top with the remaining cheese shreds and garnish with a sprinkle of smoked paprika on top of each. Broil the stuffed skins for 5 to 7 minutes or until the cheese is melted and bubbling. Garnish with additional chives just before serving.

If you're reserving the mashed potato mixture for another use, brush the baked skins with a thin layer of onion dip, layer cheese shreds, the chives, pickled jalapeños, and more cheese shreds, and then garnish with smoked paprika. Broil for 5 to 8 minutes, until the cheese is melted and the skins are crispy.

HOT TIP If you want to make your shishito peppers into more of a meal, try **Blistered Shishito Peppers with Ramen (page 168)**. And if you want to make **Warm Shishito Pepper Dip (page 173)**, reserve 13 to 15 blistered peppers.

BLISTERED SHISHITO PEPPERS

2 mins.   10 mins.

use Sesame Ginger Sauce (page 192)

INGREDIENTS

1   tablespoon avocado oil or neutral vegetable oil

3   cups shishito peppers (30 to 32 peppers)

    Maldon sea salt flakes or coarse sea salt, to taste

1   lemon or lime, halved

1   batch Sesame Ginger Sauce, for dipping

    Sesame seeds, for garnish

MAKES 4 TO 6 SERVINGS (ABOUT 3 CUPS OF PEPPERS) The first time I had these was at a restaurant in New Orleans. I wondered why the hell I had never heard of them before. They were delicious little snacks that were fun and easy to eat. You know what else is fun about them? The peppers are mostly mild, but in every batch there's bound to be one or two real hot ones (don't ask why; it's nature). So that's also a fun game to play when you serve them at your next shindig: whoever gets the hot one has to wash the dishes!

To a large cast-iron pan over medium-high heat, add the oil.

Cook the peppers in two batches so you can blister them in one layer. Once the oil is hot, add the first batch of peppers and cook for about 2 minutes per side, until the skin is blistered and they've turned a brighter green.

Remove the peppers from the pan and garnish with the salt immediately. Repeat with the remaining batch of peppers. The heat can be lowered a bit if the oil is smoking, since the cast iron will be quite hot by the second batch.

If you want to caramelize the lemon or lime halves for serving, place the halves cut-side-down into the empty pan. It will take about 2 minutes to get the flesh golden brown and caramelized.

Serve the peppers with the sesame ginger sauce garnished with sesame seeds and the charred lemon or lime halves. Squeeze the juice on the peppers just before consuming.

BLISTERED SHISHITO PEPPERS WITH RAMEN

 10 mins. 30 mins.

use Blistered Shishito Peppers (page 167)

Sesame Ginger Sauce (page 192)

INGREDIENTS

1	package (18 oz/450 g fresh or 10.5 oz/300 g dry) ramen noodles
2	cups shredded napa cabbage
1	cup shredded purple cabbage
½	cup finely chopped green onion (white and light green parts)
1	teaspoon toasted sesame oil
½	teaspoon sea salt
	Pinch of chili flakes
3	cups Blistered Shishito Peppers
1	batch Sesame Ginger Sauce
	Sesame seeds, for garnish

MAKES 3 TO 4 SERVINGS This dish is super simple, but it's a nice way to take your freshly blistered or leftover shishitos and turn them into a whole hearty meal. And who doesn't love ramen?! If you can find the fresh (and vegan-friendly) Japanese kind, it'll make this meal that much better, but I know the dry instant ones are very common. They'll work, too, but chances are you'll have to toss the flavor packet since those aren't usually vegan. You could also make this with chow mein, soba, or rice vermicelli.

Cook the noodles until al dente according to package directions. Drain but do not rinse.

Heat the same cast-iron pan you just made the shishito peppers in over medium heat and sauté the cabbages and green onion in the sesame oil, sea salt, and chili flakes for about 3 minutes, until just softened. If reheating leftover shishito peppers, toss them in at the end just to warm them through.

Toss the drained noodles with ¼ cup of the sesame ginger sauce. Add the noodles to a plate, top with the cabbage mixture and the peppers, and garnish with sesame seeds. Drizzle with more sesame ginger sauce for serving.

stuff to make...for a potluck (or other BYOVD event—bring your own vegan dish event)

I'm well versed in having to pick up the missing vegan-friendly pieces when going to a potluck or other gathering where the host (or your mother) doesn't know what to make you! It's all good. I'm more than happy to bring one of my stellar vegan recipes to the table so *everyone* can enjoy and hopefully be turned on to that vegan life in the process!

I NEED AN APPIE!

My go-to's would be the **Savory Cheese Tart (page 177)**, **Sweet & Sour Rice Balls (page 186)**, or the **Warm Shishito Pepper Dip (page 173)** for something more fancy, or any of the **HFF Snack Mixes (pages 178–183)** and the **Classic Onion Dip (page 163)** if you're hanging with friends!

I NEED AN IMPRESSIVE MAIN DISH!

HFF Famous Bowls (page 153)

You can easily bring all the components already made, then just reheat and serve. If it's not a potluck and you're bringing this to Thanksgiving for you and boo, heads up...bring extra, 'cause everyone is about to drop their jaws and hover over your plate wondering what the heck you're eating... and ask if they can have some!

Sloppy Joe Zucchini Boats (page 145) or Kabocha Stuffed Shells (page 130)

These are good, easy options you can make the day or morning of, cover with foil, transport with ease, and then bake an hour or so before dinner commences. You can also use these as an excuse "to check on your dinner" and get out of the awkward convo you're having with *whomever* you haven't seen in forever!

I NEED A DESSERT!

You def need something easy and that'll serve a lot of people, so I'd go with the **Chocolate Peanut Butter Krispie Cake (page 222)** or the **Rocky Road Bars (page 205)**. If you can't bring peanuts, go with one of my **Loaf Cakes (pages 214–219)**. Dessert slayed!

WARM SHISHITO PEPPER DIP

 15 mins. 20 mins.

use Blistered Shishito Peppers (page 167)

INGREDIENTS

13–15 Blistered Shishito Peppers, stems removed (reserve 3 to 5 peppers for garnish/dipping)

2 cups vegan mozzarella shreds

1 cup vegan sour cream

½ cup vegan mayonnaise

2 tablespoons nutritional yeast

2 tablespoons coarsely chopped chives

1 teaspoon lime zest (about 1 lime)

2 tablespoons lime juice (about 1 lime)

1 tablespoon hot sauce

1 teaspoon apple cider vinegar

1 teaspoon onion powder

1 teaspoon sea salt

1 teaspoon ground black pepper

1 large garlic clove

Your fave chips, crackers, or vegetables, for serving

MAKES 4 TO 6 SERVINGS (2 TO 2½ CUPS) This dip is gonna blow your mind! It's warm, creamy, and tangy—it kind of reminds me of crab dip, which is odd since shishitos are nothing like crab at all. You'll need about half the batch of blistered shishitos to make this party-size appie, and it's something you can make a day ahead and then bake right before serving. Don't have the shishito peppers? You can replace 'em with 1 cup of marinated artichokes for a warm artichoke dip instead.

Preheat the oven to 425°F.

In a food processor, add 10 of the blistered peppers, 1 cup of the vegan mozzarella shreds, the sour cream, mayonnaise, nutritional yeast, chives, lime zest and juice, hot sauce, apple cider vinegar, onion powder, sea salt, black pepper, and garlic. Pulse until well combined and mostly smooth. It will have a bit of texture to it.

Transfer the dip to an oven-safe dish and top with the remaining 1 cup of mozzarella shreds. Bake for 15 minutes, until the sides are bubbling and the top is browned. Broil for 5 minutes if necessary to get the top properly browned and crispy.

Garnish with the reserved blistered peppers on top and serve with chips, crackers, or vegetables of your choice.

SMOKY CHEESE SPREAD

15 mins.   8–12 mins.

overnight refrigeration

INGREDIENTS

1	cup raw whole cashews or roasted unsalted cashews
½	cup peeled white or yellow potato, cut into 1-inch cubes
2	tablespoons tapioca flour
1	tablespoon coarsely chopped roasted red peppers from a jar
2	teaspoons mellow white miso
2	teaspoons apple cider vinegar
1	teaspoon yellow mustard
1	teaspoon sea salt
1	teaspoon smoked paprika
¼	teaspoon garlic powder
¼	teaspoon white pepper

MAKES ABOUT 1½ CUPS I've always wanted a spreadable orange vegan cheese I can eat with buttery crackers. Yeah, exactly, think Cheez Whiz but made with respectable ingredients. Well, this is it! This slightly smoky cheese is creamy and spreadable, entirely rich, and most definitely addictive. You're going to eat it off a spoon, smother sourdough toast with it, and possibly dip veggies in it, too. But I also came up with a fancy application for it . . . just flip the page to check out the **Savory Cheese Tart (page 177)**!

If using raw cashews, preheat the oven to 325°F. Toast the cashews in an even layer on a baking sheet for 12 to 14 minutes, until lightly golden brown. Set aside to cool.

In a small pot, cover the potatoes with water and bring to a boil. Cook for about 8 minutes, or until fork tender. Reserve ½ cup of the potato cooking water, drain the potatoes, and set aside.

In a high-powered blender, blend the roasted cashews into a smooth-ish cashew butter. It might still be chunky, but get it broken down as much as you can. You'll need to stop the blender and push the mixture with a spatula toward the blades a few times. Add the potatoes, reserved potato cooking water, tapioca flour, roasted red peppers, miso, apple cider vinegar, yellow mustard, sea salt, smoked paprika, garlic powder, and white pepper and blend again until very, very smooth.

Add this mixture to a small saucepan over medium-low heat. Whisk constantly for about 2 minutes, until thick and slightly lumpy. Immediately transfer back to the blender (no need to clean) and blend until thick, smooth, and creamy. Transfer to an airtight jar and set overnight in the fridge.

Use as a spread on crackers or bread or as a dip for celery or any veggies you like. Consume within 10 days.

HOT TIP If you opened a brand-new jar of roasted red peppers for this recipe, you can use up the remaining amount to make the **Kabocha Stuffed Shells (page 130)**. Or use canned fire-roasted tomatoes in place of the roasted red peppers. You can also use ½ cup of store-bought roasted cashew butter in place of the 1 cup raw or roasted whole cashews.

SAVORY CHEESE TART

 35 mins.  16–18 mins.

C 8 hrs. refrigeration

use Smoky Cheese Spread (page 174)

MAKES 16 SQUARES OR 8 RECTANGLES This is homemade vegan cheese-and-crackers rolled into one, but it's far from basic. It's the kind of thing you'll want to break out at the holidays or for a fancy party. It's heavenly! The rosemary shortbread crust on the bottom is elevated by the Smoky Cheese Spread, and your nut-and-seed topping can be anything you choose. I like the pop of green pistachios and pumpkin seeds; they're pretty and they complement the sweet currants you get in every nibble.

ROSEMARY SHORTBREAD CRUST

- ½ cup (1 stick) chilled vegan butter, cut into large chunks
- ½ cup gluten-free all-purpose flour
- ½ cup fine almond flour
- ½ cup shredded vegan Parmesan
- 2 tablespoons nutritional yeast
- 1 tablespoon finely chopped fresh rosemary
- 1 teaspoon baking powder
- ½ teaspoon onion powder
- ¼ teaspoon sea salt

TOPPINGS

- 1 batch Smoky Cheese Spread, at room temperature
- ¼ cup finely chopped salted shelled pistachios
- ¼ cup roasted salted sunflower seeds
- ¼ cup toasted pumpkin seeds
- ¼ cup dried currants

Line a 9 by 9-inch metal baking pan with 2 pieces of parchment paper that are 9 inches wide. Criss-cross them in the pan to line all sides.

To make the crust, in a food processor combine the vegan butter, GF all-purpose flour, almond flour, vegan Parmesan, nutritional yeast, rosemary, baking powder, onion powder, and sea salt and blend until the dough comes together and pulls off the sides of the processor bowl.

Using a spatula, transfer the dough onto the parchment-lined pan. Use your hands to press the dough into a flat, even layer, filling the bottom of the pan. Refrigerate this for 20 minutes.

Preheat the oven to 350°F. Bake the chilled crust for 16 to 18 minutes, until the edges are just golden brown. Allow to cool completely.

Spread the cheese spread in an even layer on the crust. The cheese spread can be freshly made and cooled to room temperature or previously made and brought to room temperature. Mix the nuts, seeds, and currants in a dish and then sprinkle in an even layer onto the cheese, gently pressing them into the top.

If the cheese spread hasn't previously set in the fridge overnight, ensure the cheese tart sits for at least 8 hours in the fridge before slicing and serving. Store leftovers in the fridge and consume within a couple days for peak freshness.

HFF SNACK MIXES 5 WAYS

PINK BEET CARAMEL

Popcorn is my desert-island food. One, it's nutritious, and I'm pretty sure you could survive on it for a while, and two, it's just delicious stuff. Of course, if you were stranded on a desert island, you'd never have this many tasty flavors to choose from, but that scenario is never going to happen so just forget about it. But maybe you're like me and all you want for dinner sometimes is popcorn. There's no shame in that since you're about to level up your popcorn game big-time. Make the seasonings and have them in your cupboard at the ready or add these awesome mix-ins to really kick your popcorn snacks up a notch! Homemade popcorn should be eaten immediately and not stored, as it gets stale very quickly, so make all of these snack mixes fresh. The seasoning mixes can be stored in a jar or airtight container for 2 months in a cool, dry place.

Continued

DILL PICKLE

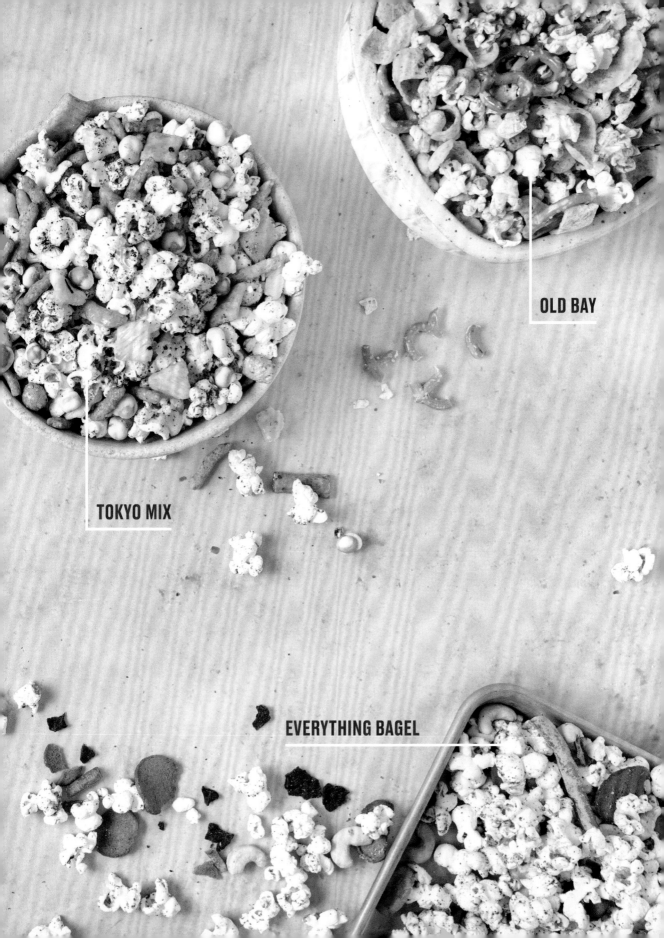

OLD BAY

TOKYO MIX

EVERYTHING BAGEL

HFF SNACK MIXES 5 WAYS

Continued

HOMEMADE STOVE-TOP POPCORN

 1 min.   8 mins.

INGREDIENTS

2   tablespoons coconut oil

½   cup organic popcorn kernels (see hot tip page 179)

¼   cup melted coconut oil or vegan butter (not required for Pink Beet Caramel Popcorn)

Popcorn seasoning of choice

MAKES ABOUT 11 CUPS POPCORN It's best not to pop more than ½ cup of kernels as instructed or you'll end up with burnt or unpopped corn. If you want more, just make 2 batches separately.

To make the popcorn, heat a large pot over medium-high heat with the coconut oil and 1 popcorn kernel. Place a tight-fitting lid on the pot, and when you hear the kernel pop after 4 or 5 minutes, pour the remaining kernels into the pot and place the lid back on. Lower the heat to medium. Wearing oven mitts, shake the pot a few times just over the burner and place it back down. Allow some steam to escape by moving the lid to the side, leaving a crack open for a moment. Place the lid back on and you should hear the kernels begin popping fairly quickly. Continue shaking the pot periodically while it's popping to prevent the popcorn from burning. It will take about 3 minutes to pop all the corn. If the popcorn doesn't pop continuously and pretty vigorously, you might have stale popcorn kernels!

As soon as the popping has stopped, remove the pot from the heat and keep the lid on, as some kernels may still pop. Allow the pot to cool off quite a bit before adding the seasoning—otherwise the seasoning mixes will burn. Or you can transfer the popped corn to another large pot to mix in the oil or butter and seasoning.

Add the melted coconut oil or butter and the amount of seasoning mix indicated for whichever flavor you're making. Stir to coat or place the lid back on the pot and shake the pot around vigorously to coat the popcorn. If you're making the caramel popcorn, make the beet caramel while the popcorn cools.

Eat the seasoned popcorn on its own or level up and add in the snack mix options.

EVERYTHING BAGEL POPCORN SEASONING + SNACK MIX

 10 mins.

SEASONING (MAKES ABOUT ⅔ CUP)

- 1½   tablespoons poppy seeds
- 1½   tablespoons sesame seeds
- 1½   tablespoons raw or roasted sunflower seeds
- 1½   tablespoons dried minced onion
- 1   tablespoon granulated garlic powder
- 1   teaspoon sea salt

LEVEL UP WITH SNACK MIX OPTIONS (PER BATCH OF POPCORN)

- 2   cups rye bagel chips
- 2   cups dehydrated vegetable chips
- 1   cup roasted salted cashews

This seasoning mix is EVERYTHING! You can also use it on fancy toasts or as a topping on your salads or grain bowls. I bet ya it's even delish on mac n' cheese!

To make the seasoning, in a clean coffee grinder or spice grinder, grind the poppy seeds, sesame seeds, sunflower seeds, dehydrated onion, garlic powder, and sea salt to a very fine powder. You may have to grind the spices in two batches. Sprinkle ⅓ cup of the spice mix over the popcorn and reserve the rest for a future batch. If adding snack mix options, add them in after you season the popcorn.

DILL PICKLE POPCORN SEASONING + SNACK MIX

 10 mins.

SEASONING (MAKES ABOUT ½ CUP)

- 3   tablespoons dill seeds
- 3   tablespoons dried dill weed
- 2   tablespoons mustard seed
- 1   tablespoon sea salt
- 1   tablespoon onion powder
- 1   tablespoon granulated garlic powder
- ½   tablespoon granulated sugar
- ½   teaspoon citric acid

LEVEL UP WITH SNACK MIX OPTIONS (PER BATCH OF POPCORN)

- 10–12 fried artichokes (see page 70)
- 3   cups jalapeño-flavored kettle chips
- 2   cups vegan-friendly cheese puffs

This is the ultimate homemade popcorn seasoning. Until now, I've never used citric acid or dill seeds, but both are necessary to get that characteristic tang you'd expect in a dill pickle–flavored popcorn. You're going to make this a lot, so it's worth the investment.

To make the seasoning, in a clean coffee grinder or spice grinder, grind the dill seeds, dill weed, mustard seed, sea salt, onion powder, garlic powder, sugar, and citric acid to a very fine powder. You may have to grind the spices in two batches. Sprinkle half of the spice mix over the popcorn and reserve the rest for a future batch. If adding snack mix options, add them in after you season the popcorn.

Continued

HFF SNACK MIXES 5 WAYS

Continued

SEASONING (MAKES ABOUT ½ CUP)

1   package (35 oz/10 g) or
    2 large sheets roasted salted
    seaweed snacks

2   tablespoons dried minced onion

2   tablespoons mixed black and white
    sesame seeds

1½ tablespoons nutritional yeast

1   teaspoon sea salt

LEVEL UP WITH SNACK MIX OPTIONS (PER BATCH OF POPCORN)

3   cups rice sembei snacks

2   cups sesame sticks

1   cup natural wasabi peas

TOKYO MIX POPCORN SEASONING + SNACK MIX

 10 mins.

This popcorn mix is so unique you'll want to show it off to everyone you know! I've found myself also using it on rice or noodle bowls, since it's kind of like a leveled-up gomashio or furikake. After using it for one batch of popcorn, I suggest using the rest to make the **Tokyo Street Fries (page 185)**.

Use a clean coffee grinder or spice grinder to grind the ingredients to a very fine powder. First grind the roasted seaweed snacks in batches by adding torn pieces to the grinder to get them into small pieces. The seaweed snacks have additional oil, so they will stick to the sides of the grinder. You might need to stop and start the grinder to push the pieces toward the blade and continue pulsing. Pour into a bowl when each batch is finished. Then add all the small pieces of seaweed back into the grinder with the dried minced onion, sesame seeds, nutritional yeast, and sea salt and pulse to a fine powder. You may have to do this in two batches. Sprinkle half the spice mix over the popcorn and reserve the rest for a future batch. If adding snack mix options, add them in after you season the popcorn.

SEASONING (MAKES ABOUT ⅓ CUP)

¼   cup + 1 tablespoon nutritional yeast

2   tablespoons Old Bay Seasoning

1   teaspoon onion powder

½   teaspoon sea salt

LEVEL UP WITH SNACK MIX OPTIONS (PER BATCH OF POPCORN)

3   cups Fritos

2   cups mini pretzels

1   cup spicy peanuts

OLD BAY POPCORN SEASONING + SNACK MIX

 10 mins.

This seasoning mix is quite concentrated in flavor, so you don't need to use a lot to coat the popcorn. Adjust to your personal taste.

To make the seasoning, in a clean coffee grinder or spice grinder, grind the nutritional yeast, Old Bay, onion powder, and sea salt to a very fine powder. You may have to grind the spices in two batches. Sprinkle 1½ tablespoons of the spice mix over the popcorn and reserve the rest for future batches. If adding snack mix options, add them in after you season the popcorn.

PINK BEET CARAMEL POPCORN + SNACK MIX

⬦ 30 mins. 🍲 75 mins.

BEET CARAMEL

- ¼ cup frozen or peeled fresh beet chunks
- ½ cup canned full-fat coconut milk, at room temperature, plus more as needed
- 1 teaspoon vanilla extract
- ½ teaspoon sea salt
- ¼ cup melted vegan butter
- ¾ cup granulated sugar

LEVEL UP WITH SNACK MIX OPTIONS (PER BATCH OF POPCORN)

- 1 cup salted shelled pistachios
- 1 cup Unreal dark chocolate crispy gems
- ½ cup dried blueberries

MAKES ABOUT 11 CUPS This is the only popcorn that has a different process—you have to make the popcorn and caramel at the same time. Do not premake the caramel and think you can store it and then add it to the popcorn later; it will get too stiff or even crystallize, which doesn't make for nice, shiny pink kernels! For the brightest pink results, use frozen beet chunks or peeled raw beet. Do not use pickled or cooked beets, as this will muddy up the color and flavor.

If using frozen beets, ensure they are fully thawed and soft before making the caramel. Drain off any excess pooled liquid and place the beets in a high-powered blender. Add the coconut milk, vanilla, and sea salt and combine until mostly smooth. Frozen thawed beets will have enough moisture to blend this smooth, but if you're using fresh raw beets, you might need to add some more coconut milk/water from the can to help liquefy the mixture.

Slowly add the melted butter while blending on low speed. Blend until very smooth and no visible pieces of beet remain. Add to a saucepan with the sugar and place over medium heat. Whisk constantly as it comes to a vigorous simmer, about 4 minutes. Once it's bubbling and foamy, rising in the saucepan, reduce the heat to medium-low and continue whisking constantly for another 4 minutes, until it's glossy and thicker and can coat the side of the saucepan. A thermometer should read 210 to 220°F. Let the caramel rest off the heat for about 15 minutes.

Preheat the oven to 250°F. Line 2 large baking sheets with Silpat mats or parchment paper.

Drizzle the caramel over the cooled popcorn in the pot and stir immediately to coat all the kernels. Divide the popcorn between the baking sheets and spread out in an even layer. Bake for 1 hour, tossing about every 20 minutes. Transfer the baking sheets to wire racks and let the popcorn cool completely before eating.

If adding snack mix options, add them into the cooled and dried caramel popcorn.

TOKYO STREET FRIES

 5 mins.   25 mins.

use Tokyo Mix Popcorn Seasoning (page 182)

INGREDIENTS

1	package (about 20 oz/567 g) frozen shoestring fries
⅓	cup vegan mayonnaise
1	tablespoon Sriracha
¼	cup Tokyo Mix Popcorn Seasoning
¼	cup finely chopped green onion (white and light green parts)
1	teaspoon black sesame seeds

MAKES 2 LARGE OR 4 SMALL SERVINGS This is a genius way to use the Tokyo Mix Popcorn Seasoning again and again, since you won't be able to get enough of it! Instead of using convenient frozen fries, you can make the wedges in **Fries & Salad (page 80)**. But I love quick frozen french fries. In fact, my friends make fun of me because I can't seem to go three or four days without eating french fries. Is that a problem? I think it's a good problem, personally. I've included a simple Sriracha mayo to drizzle on these fries, but in the event that you have some **Gochujang Aioli (page 191)** left over, feel free to use that instead.

Preheat the oven to 425°F.

Lay out the frozen fries on a baking sheet in an even layer and bake for 20 to 25 minutes, or according to package directions, until golden brown and crispy.

In a small bowl, combine the vegan mayonnaise and Sriracha.

When the fries are baked, immediately transfer to a large bowl and toss with the popcorn seasoning.

Transfer the fries to a serving platter, drizzle with the Sriracha mayo, and sprinkle the green onion and sesame seeds on top.

SWEET & SOUR RICE BALLS

 45 mins.   35–55 mins.

C 2 hrs. refrigeration

RICE BALLS

1	cup short-grain brown rice (or 3 cups cooked)
2	tablespoons vegan butter
1½	cups finely chopped white or yellow onion (about 1 large onion)
¼	cup finely chopped shallot (about 1 shallot)
2	tablespoons minced garlic (3 or 4 large cloves)
1	teaspoon chili flakes
2	cups packed baby spinach, finely chopped
½	cup packed fresh basil, finely chopped
½	cup packed parsley, finely chopped
½	teaspoon sea salt
½	teaspoon ground black pepper
2	tablespoons unseasoned rice vinegar
1	tablespoon coconut sugar
1	tablespoon gluten-free tamari or soy sauce
2	cups vegan mozzarella shreds
2	tablespoons golden flax meal
½	cup water
1	cup gluten-free all-purpose flour
1	cup gluten-free panko-style bread crumbs
2	cups neutral vegetable oil, for frying

MAKES 22 TO 24 RICE BALLS Arancini meets Chinese takeout! Savory cheesy rice balls coated in a crispy breading and dunked in sweet & sour sauce…have you heard of such a thing? I had a similar version of these at Erewhon, an over-the-top luxury grocery store in LA, where you might just see some celebs. (I was just there for the novelty, of course.) Anyway, they were delicious, and like any good taste tester and recipe developer, I ate them a couple more times to deconstruct and dissect so I could take a stab at 'em myself.

To make the rice balls, cook the rice according to the package directions. You can also use leftover rice.

Heat a large cast-iron pan over medium heat and add the butter. Once it's melted, add the onion, shallot, garlic, and chili flakes. Stir occasionally, cooking for 5 minutes, until very soft.

Add the spinach, basil, parsley, sea salt, and black pepper and cook for another 1 to 2 minutes, until soft and wilted. Add the rice vinegar, coconut sugar, and tamari or soy sauce and stir to combine. Add the cooked rice and cheese shreds and stir frequently until the cheese is just melted and looking gooey, 8 to 9 minutes. Transfer the mixture to a bowl and refrigerate for about 1 hour, until the mixture is cool enough to handle. Clean out the cast-iron pan, as you will use it to fry the rice balls.

While the rice mixture is cooling, make the sweet & sour sauce. In a small bowl combine the cornstarch and 2 teaspoons water and set aside.

Heat a saucepan with oil over medium-low heat. Once the oil is hot, add the garlic, ginger, and chili flakes. Stir for 1 minute, until fragrant, being careful not to burn the garlic or ginger. Add the sugar, ½ cup water, vinegar, tomato paste, and tamari or soy sauce and whisk constantly over medium heat until just bubbling. Whisk in the cornstarch mixture and whisk frequently while it continues to bubble for 6 minutes, until thickened, glossy, and reduced. Set aside to cool.

Use a Silpat mat or parchment paper to line a large baking sheet. Have a bowl of water on hand. Lightly wet your hands. Measure about 2 tablespoons of the cooled rice mixture and form a ball by gently tossing it back and forth between your palms. Place it on the baking sheet. Continue making all the rice balls and then

SWEET & SOUR SAUCE (MAKES 1 CUP)

2	teaspoons cornstarch (can substitute tapioca or arrowroot)
2	teaspoons water
2	teaspoons neutral vegetable oil
2	teaspoons minced garlic (1 or 2 large cloves)
1	teaspoon peeled and minced fresh ginger
½	teaspoon chili flakes
½	cup granulated sugar
½	cup water
⅓	cup unseasoned rice vinegar
1	tablespoon tomato paste
1	tablespoon gluten-free tamari or low-sodium soy sauce

refrigerate them on the sheet for at least 1 hour, until totally cooled and more firm.

Combine the flax meal and ½ cup water in a bowl and set aside to thicken for about 10 minutes. In another bowl, add the flour, and in another bowl, add the bread crumbs. Line a plate with a paper towel.

Add the frying oil to the large cast-iron pan and heat to about 360°F. Dredge a rice ball in the flour, then coat in the flax-meal mixture, and then coat well in the bread crumbs. Fry the rice balls in batches for 3 to 4 minutes, flipping once to fry evenly. Remove the rice balls with a slotted spoon and transfer to the prepared plate.

Warm your sweet & sour sauce if needed before serving. Serve the sauce on the side for dipping or spoon the sauce right over the rice balls to coat them more. Serve immediately.

Reheat leftover sweet & sour sauce over medium-low heat in a saucepan, whisking until warmed through. If needed, add a small amount of water to get the right consistency.

EGG YOLK SAUCE

5 mins. 10 mins.

INGREDIENTS

2	Campari/cocktail tomatoes or 4 grape tomatoes
¼	cup melted vegan butter + 2 tablespoons solid vegan butter
¼	cup water
¼	cup unsweetened nondairy milk
¼	cup nutritional yeast
1	teaspoon cornstarch (can substitute tapioca or arrowroot)
½	teaspoon ground turmeric
½	teaspoon kala namak

MAKES ABOUT 1 CUP Here's your saucy staple for breakfast stuff of all kinds. You saw it used throughout the breakfast chapter, binding the filling for the **Stuffed Breakfast Danishes (page 24)** like a champ and creating an ooey-gooey topping for **Breakfast Za (page 20)**, but sometimes I like it in its purest and simplest form. Just like a runny egg yolk, it's great straight up on some crunchy toast with a little fried tofu egg white. Cut a brick of medium-firm or firm tofu into thin slices on the widest side, just like in the **Clubhouse Sandwich (page 66)**. You can cut it into a round if you want, and then fry it in a cast-iron pan with a bit of oil until it's bubbling and gets a little crispy on the edges. Season with salt and pepper, flip, and fry the other side. Then place it on the toast and drizzle it with as much egg yolk sauce as you can handle.

Cut the tomatoes in half and use your hands to scoop out the watery inside and seeds, which you'll either discard or save to throw in the **Tortilla Soup (page 46)** or the **Ragu Bolognese (page 122)**.

In a high-powered blender, add the tomato pieces with the melted vegan butter, water, nondairy milk, nutritional yeast, cornstarch, and turmeric and blend on high until very smooth. Transfer to a saucepan and whisk over medium heat until it thickens, 4 to 5 minutes. Once it's bubbling and thicker, remove the saucepan from the heat. Just before serving, whisk in the solid vegan butter and the kala namak.

This is best made as fresh as possible and consumed within 1 or 2 days.

HOT TIP Heating kala namak will diminish the "eggy" flavor and smell, so if you're making this to use on any breakfast item ahead of time, blend it and heat it through to thicken it. Just before serving, add the vegan butter and kala namak.

CILANTRO SOUR CREAM

 5 mins. Ⓒ 20 mins. soaking

INGREDIENTS

½   cup raw whole cashews

¼   cup unsweetened nondairy milk

⅓   cup packed fresh cilantro

3   tablespoons fresh lime juice
    (about 2 limes)

2   teaspoons apple cider vinegar

½   teaspoon garlic powder

½   teaspoon sea salt

MAKES ABOUT ⅔ CUP Of course, you can make this sour cream plain and tangy without cilantro (you hater), but if you LOVE cilantro like me, then this will be your new fave thing to dollop on everything you eat! This recipe makes as much as you'll need for one recipe in this book, like the **Butter Chicken Nachos (page 159)** or **Breakfast Totchos (page 23),** but it's easy to double or triple if you want to keep some for more recipes throughout the week.

Soak the cashews in boiling-hot water for 20 minutes. Drain the cashews and discard the water.

In a high-powered blender, combine the cashews, nondairy milk, cilantro, lime juice, apple cider vinegar, garlic powder, and sea salt. Blend until very smooth.

Transfer to a squeeze bottle, if desired, and use immediately as a drizzle. If you want a firmer sour cream to dollop, refrigerate the mixture in a glass jar or container for a few hours or overnight.

This keeps up to 7 days in the fridge, but for best results, use immediately. This isn't the best sauce to freeze and keep for longer storage.

JALAPEÑO RANCH

 10 mins.

INGREDIENTS

¾	cup vegan mayonnaise
3	tablespoons pickled jalapeños in brine (about 10 slices including brine)
1	tablespoon lime juice (about half a lime)
1	tablespoon coarsely chopped fresh dill
1	tablespoon coarsely chopped chives
1	teaspoon onion powder
½	teaspoon ground black pepper
¼	teaspoon sea salt

MAKES ABOUT 1 CUP K, you already know I'm a ranch fiend, so throwing some spicy jalapeños in the mix is just an obvious choice. In addition to all the wonderful recipes I've drizzled this on in the book, this Jalapeño Ranch is gonna kick up all kinds of taco creations and take veggies and dip to a new level in your life.

In a high-powered blender or small food processor combine the vegan mayonnaise, pickled jalapeños, lime juice, dill, chives, onion powder, black pepper, and sea salt and blend until very smooth.

Alternatively, you can finely chop the jalapeños and herbs and combine the ingredients in a bowl or jar.

Store in the fridge for up to 10 days.

HOT TIP You can also use fresh jalapeños if you want. Use 3 tablespoons of finely minced fresh jalapeño and include half the seeds for more spice, if desired. Also add 2 teaspoons white vinegar and ½ teaspoon sea salt to replace the brine of the pickled version.

GOCHUJANG AIOLI

 5 mins.

INGREDIENTS

¾ cup vegan mayonnaise

2 tablespoons lemon juice
   (about 1 lemon)

1 tablespoon store-bought
   vegan kimchi

1 tablespoon kimchi brine

1 tablespoon coarsely chopped chives

1 large garlic clove

1 teaspoon gochujang (use more
   for hot)

½ teaspoon ground black pepper

MAKES ABOUT 1 CUP Gochujang is my *flavorite*! That's not a typo. It's my new fave flavor, and this easy aioli gets an extra kick from kimchi, too. This spicy aioli is smeared all over the **Korean BBQ Burritos (page 140)**, but I want you to get adventurous and start putting it into regular rotation in your arsenal of homemade hot for food condiments!

In a high-powered blender combine the vegan mayonnaise, lemon juice, kimchi, kimchi brine, chives, garlic, gochujang, and black pepper and blend until smooth. Alternatively, you can finely chop the kimchi, chives, and garlic and combine the ingredients in a bowl or jar.

Store in the fridge and consume within 2 weeks.

SESAME GINGER SAUCE

 10 mins. 5 mins.

INGREDIENTS

¼ cup gluten-free tamari or low-sodium soy sauce

¼ cup water

2 tablespoons unseasoned rice vinegar

2 tablespoons toasted sesame oil

2 tablespoons granulated sugar

2 tablespoons peeled and coarsely chopped fresh ginger

2 tablespoons coarsely chopped garlic (2 or 3 large cloves)

1 tablespoon coarsely chopped chives

1 teaspoon cornstarch (can substitute tapioca or arrowroot)

½ teaspoon white pepper (can substitute ground black pepper)

Sesame seeds, for garnish (optional)

MAKES ABOUT ¾ CUP This sauce is a perfectly balanced condiment for Asian-inspired recipes. It's infused with lots of fresh ginger, which makes it a zingy pairing for more than just the **Blistered Shishito Peppers (page 167)** or its corresponding ramen creation (page 168). You can use it as a dip for the **All-Green Fresh Rolls (page 160)** or a fried spring roll creation. Or dip some sesame-crusted cauliflower wings into it. Use my famous blog recipe for that one, folks!

In a high-powered blender combine the tamari or soy sauce, water, rice vinegar, sesame oil, sugar, ginger, garlic, chives, cornstarch, and white pepper and blend until smooth.

Transfer to a small saucepan over medium heat and bring to a low simmer, 2 to 3 minutes, stirring occasionally. Turn the heat down to low and whisk constantly while the sauce thickens up and turns glossy, about another 3 minutes. Garnish with the sesame seeds before serving.

If reheating leftovers, you might need to add a splash of water to get the sauce to a smooth, dippable consistency again. Store in the fridge and consume within 7 days.

PUMPKIN MISO GRAVY

5 mins. 10 mins.

INGREDIENTS

2   teaspoons vegan chicken-flavored bouillon base or 2 cubes

2   cups hot water (or hot vegetable stock, if not using bouillon base or cubes)

1   cup canned pure pumpkin puree

2   tablespoons nutritional yeast

2   tablespoons gluten-free tamari or low-sodium soy sauce

1   tablespoon mellow white miso

¼   cup vegan butter

¼   cup gluten-free all-purpose flour

MAKES ABOUT 3 CUPS This is the closest thing I've tasted to a vegan chicken or turkey gravy, but of course, sans meat drippings! Ew. Why pumpkin, you're wondering? Well, it creates a nice color and the right amount of thickness and starch for a gravy, plus it's a cozy ingredient and has some nutritional value, too. There's only a subtle hint of it by the time I round this out with some umami bombs. If you're using vegetable stock as a substitute for the bouillon and hot water, be sure to bring it to a boil before adding it to the blender with the other ingredients.

In a high-powered blender combine the bouillon base, water, pumpkin puree, nutritional yeast, tamari or soy sauce, and miso and blend until very smooth.

Heat a cast-iron pan over medium heat with the vegan butter. Let it melt and start to come to a bubble. Sprinkle the flour in gradually while whisking vigorously to incorporate the flour. Once the flour is mostly mixed in and no longer lumpy, switch to using a wooden roux spoon or heat-safe spatula with a flat end and continuously push the mixture around for 4 to 5 minutes, until it turns a light brown color, almost like you put too much cream in your coffee. Turn the heat down to low while continuing to push the mixture around for 1 more minute. Go back to using the whisk while you gradually pour the blended mixture into the pan. It will splash a little as the roux will be very hot, but keep whisking to prevent lumps until it's all well combined. Continue whisking another 2 minutes, until the gravy is velvety and smooth.

The gravy may form a skin, which can easily be whisked in when you're reheating. If the gravy has thickened too much, add a bit of water or stock when reheating it. Refrigerate leftovers and consume within 5 days.

CRISPY ONION STRINGS

14 mins. | 20–30 mins.

INGREDIENTS

1	large white onion, peeled
3	cups neutral vegetable oil, for frying
1½	cups unsweetened soy milk
1	tablespoon apple cider vinegar
2	cups all-purpose flour
1½	teaspoons smoked paprika
1	teaspoon granulated garlic powder
1	teaspoon sea salt, plus more for finishing
½	teaspoon cayenne pepper
½	teaspoon ground black pepper

MAKES 5 TO 6 CUPS If you're a member of the hot for food fam, meaning you've been with me a while, you're already quite familiar with crispy onion strings! These delicate beauties are the perfect companion to lots of stuff, like stacked burgers and sandwiches. You could throw them on soups, in pasta salads at a BBQ, or alongside a juicy mushroom or tofu steak. Yum! They're perfect multitaskers and even better, you can freeze them and have them ready to add crunchy satisfaction to any meal, any time.

Thinly slice the onion. It's best to use a mandoline (with the hand guard!) to get the slices even, but if you have great knife skills, then try it by hand. The slices should be thin enough that you can almost see through them.

Heat up the frying oil in a heavy-bottom pot or a deep fryer to 365 to 375°F. Using 3 cups is a suggestion. If using a deep fryer, you may need more to reach the fill line of the vessel, and if you're using a pot, be sure it's only a third full of oil.

Meanwhile, in a shallow dish, whisk together the soy milk and apple cider vinegar. Add the onion slices and let them soak for 15 minutes. In a separate mixing bowl, combine the flour with the smoked paprika, garlic powder, sea salt, cayenne, and black pepper.

When the oil is the right temperature, use your hand or a pair of tongs to take a small handful of onion slices from the liquid and evenly coat with the flour mixture. Place the onions into the oil. Use a fork to move them around in the oil to prevent any from sticking to each other. Fry for about 2 minutes, until golden brown. Remove that batch with the tongs and lay onto a wire rack placed over a baking sheet. Sprinkle with a small pinch of sea salt. Continue frying in batches until the remaining onions are fried.

Once the onion strings are completely cool, you can place any leftovers in a freezer-safe bag or container for longer storage. To reheat, preheat the oven to 400°F. Lay the onions on a baking sheet and bake for 5 to 7 minutes, until crispy. Watch closely, as the onions are likely to overcook quickly and turn too dark.

HOT TIP Don't eat them all at once! Save some to make **The "Sweet" Grilled Cheese (page 106)** or get a little extra and serve these with the **Classic Onion Dip (page 163)** or **Warm Shishito Pepper Dip (page 173)**!

OLD BAY CROUTONS

 5 mins.   20 mins.

INGREDIENTS

1	small baguette, torn into large pieces (about 3 cups)
2	tablespoons extra-virgin olive oil
1	teaspoon Old Bay Seasoning
½	teaspoon granulated garlic powder
¼	teaspoon sea salt

MAKES ABOUT 3 CUPS Old Bay is the way to level up the basic crouton! There's nothing fancy going on here, but adding the savory seasoning to these chunks of bread will give them purpose for soups, chowders, and salads. It's going to be your fave seasoning, guaranteed.

Preheat the oven to 400°F.

Place the torn pieces of baguette onto a large baking sheet. Drizzle with the olive oil and sprinkle with the Old Bay, garlic powder, and sea salt. Toss and coat with your hands. Spread out the pieces in one even layer. Bake for 15 to 20 minutes, until golden brown and crispy.

Serve the croutons with a salad or soup of your choice. I suggest the **Creamy Green Pea Soup (page 52)** or **Corn Chowder (page 56)**.

TAHINI CAESAR DRESSING

SALAD DRESSINGS FOR DUMMIES

I know, you're not a dummy. It's just a way of saying these dressings are easy and foolproof, and I can't wait for you to stop using store-bought salad dressing because you deserve so much better! These range from almost too easy to slightly more laborious, but it's nothing more complicated than chopping some stuff and blending until smooth. If the dressings don't get eaten immediately, they can be stored for up to 7 days in the fridge.

USE UP THE HUMMUS DRESSING

CREAMY PESTO DRESSING

PINK GODDESS DRESSING

SESAME SOY VINAIGRETTE

SALAD DRESSINGS FOR DUMMIES

Continued

⅓ cup extra-virgin olive oil

⅓ cup lemon juice (about 3 lemons)

⅓ cup tahini

4 large garlic cloves

1 tablespoon capers + 1 tablespoon caper brine

1 tablespoon vegan Worcestershire

1 tablespoon maple syrup, agave nectar, or coconut sugar

1 tablespoon water

½ teaspoon sea salt

½ teaspoon ground black pepper

TAHINI CAESAR DRESSING

 5 mins.

MAKES ABOUT 1¼ CUPS I have a very lovely creamy cashew Caesar dressing recipe you know and love, but this one is equally as delicious and just a little simpler since it uses tahini.

In a high-powered blender, combine all of the ingredients and blend until very smooth.

PINK GODDESS DRESSING

 5–10 mins.

1 cup beet chunks

3 large garlic cloves

½ cup vegan mayonnaise

¼ cup loose-packed fresh basil leaves

¼ cup loose-packed fresh dill

¼ cup loose-packed fresh parsley

¼ cup coarsely chopped green onion or chives

2 tablespoons fresh tarragon leaves

2 tablespoons lemon juice (about 1 lemon)

½ teaspoon sea salt

½ teaspoon ground black pepper

MAKES ABOUT 1¼ CUPS You've heard of green goddess dressing, but how about pink goddess! It's so pretty and packs the nutritious punch of beets. It's best to use frozen beet chunks or peeled raw beets for this dressing, as I find the color is the brightest and prettiest. But if all you can find are jarred or canned beets, try to find ones that don't have added sugar. If they have added vinegar, then be sure you don't add the lemon juice until you taste without it and add as much as you need. If using frozen beets, defrost in a bowl of hot water for 5 to 8 minutes, until mostly thawed, and then drain the water. If using canned or jarred, drain the excess liquid before adding the beets to the blender.

In a high-powered blender, combine all of the ingredients and blend until very smooth.

SESAME SOY VINAIGRETTE

 10 mins.

½ cup gluten-free tamari or low-sodium soy sauce

¼ cup toasted sesame oil

2 tablespoons unseasoned rice vinegar

1 tablespoon Dijon mustard

2 teaspoons maple syrup or agave nectar

¼ teaspoon ground black pepper

¼ teaspoon chili flakes (optional)

MAKES ABOUT 1 CUP This dressing is super versatile and works well with a soba noodle or brown rice bowl and the **Miso-Roasted Kabocha (page 95)** in the Bowl Bible. You'll also use this as the base sauce for **Easy Tofu & Veggie Stir-Fry (page 128)** and as the dip for **Roasted Vegetable Potstickers (page 78)**.

In a high-powered blender, combine all of the ingredients and blend until very smooth.

CREAMY PESTO DRESSING

 5 mins.

⅓ cup store-bought vegan pesto

¼–½ cup water

¼ cup extra-virgin olive oil

2 tablespoons nutritional yeast

2 tablespoons lemon juice (about 1 lemon)

1 tablespoon white wine vinegar

½ teaspoon ground black pepper

¼ teaspoon sea salt

MAKES 1¼ CUPS If your store-bought pesto contains cashews, it will develop a thicker dressing, so use more water to thin that out. If your pesto doesn't have cashews (or walnuts) in it, you can start with a small amount of water and add more as needed to get your dressing creamy but pourable.

In a high-powered blender, combine all of the ingredients and blend until very smooth.

USE UP THE HUMMUS DRESSING

 5 mins.

⅓ cup store-bought hummus

2 tablespoons lemon juice (about 1 lemon)

1 tablespoon extra-virgin olive oil

1 teaspoon maple syrup

¼ teaspoon sea salt

¼ teaspoon ground black pepper

MAKES ½ CUP This is the easiest dressing of all time! It'll give you enough for about two large bowls or salads. You can easily double the recipe if you need more, but it means you'll have to spare more precious hummus.

Shake all of the ingredients together in a jar.

sweet stuff

This is the stuff I love to make the most, and I love sharing it with others. Mostly because people are happy they didn't have to make dessert themselves! But I hope this chapter gets you into the idea of making sweets without the scaries, because it's so easy. Everyone loves cookies and cake, so I bake things like coconut pecan biscotti and pumpkin loaf cake, as well as other chocolatey stuff, fried stuff, fruity stuff, and flaky stuff. I'll show you how easy it is to work with puff pastry and load it up with things like strawberries, chocolate, and almonds. Now indulge and enjoy the process of making your own sweet stuff!

ROCKY ROAD BARS

10 mins.   8 mins.

2 hrs. refrigeration

use Crunchy Coconut Granola (page 39)

INGREDIENTS

1	cup salted mini pretzels
3	bars (12 oz/339 g total) dairy-free semisweet baking chocolate, broken into squares, or 2 cups vegan chocolate chips
⅓	cup natural smooth peanut butter
½	cup mini vegan marshmallows (or halved regular-size ones)
1¾	cups Crunchy Coconut Granola
	Maldon sea salt flakes (optional)

MAKES 9 LARGE BARS OR 36 BITE-SIZE PIECES I took the Crunchy Coconut Granola from Breakfast Stuff and flipped it into this dessert, which is going to make your sweet tooth go wild! I had to put these in the freezer to stop myself from nibbling away at the entire tray. Combining the chocolate with creamy peanut butter makes the final bars the perfect consistency to sink your teeth into. I'm obsessed with all the textures going on throughout each morsel.

Line an 8 by 8-inch cake pan with parchment paper by cutting 2 strips of parchment paper, each 8 inches wide. Criss-cross them in the pan so all the sides are lined and you can easily remove the bars with the overhang of paper.

Layer the pretzels in rows in the bottom of the pan out to the edges.

To melt the chocolate, place in a heat-safe bowl over a pot with 1 to 2 inches of low simmering water. Melt the chocolate until smooth, then stir in the peanut butter until well combined and smooth.

Pour the peanut butter-chocolate mixture over the pretzels in an even layer out to the edges. Place the mini marshmallows all over the top and fill in the gaps with the granola. To really take it over the top, you could also sprinkle a pinch of Maldon sea salt flakes on top!

Refrigerate until solid, at least 2 hours. Cut into 9 squares, or, if you want bite-size pieces, cut those squares into 4 smaller squares. Store leftovers in the fridge or freezer.

CHOCOLATE CHIP CORN COOKIES

15 mins.   40 mins.

INGREDIENTS

⅔	cup frozen corn kernels
⅓	cup cold cubed vegan butter
⅓	cup granulated sugar
⅓	cup packed light brown sugar
¾	cup all-purpose flour
⅓	cup cornmeal
1	teaspoon vanilla extract
1	teaspoon lime zest (from 1 lime)
1	teaspoon baking powder
½	teaspoon baking soda
½	teaspoon sea salt
⅓	cup vegan mini chocolate chips

MAKES 20 COOKIES I know you're going to try and fight your way out of making these, claiming one shouldn't mess around with the classic chocolate chip cookie. But I'm me, so I did. This idea came from one of those rogue episodes of *RECIPE?!* on my YouTube channel and a little inspiration from dessert chain Milk Bar. I'm glad I followed my instincts. Frozen corn… crazy, but yes. Lime zest with chocolate… hell yes! I think you'll also like the fact that you make the dough entirely in a food processor. These fragrant cookies are in a league all their own, and they deserve some of the spotlight.

Preheat the oven to 350°F. Line a baking sheet with a Silpat mat or parchment paper.

In a food processor, pulse the corn kernels into a fine crumb or meal, ensuring that you stop before it becomes pureed corn!

Add the butter, granulated sugar, and brown sugar and pulse until creamed together.

Add the flour, cornmeal, vanilla, lime zest, baking powder, baking soda, and sea salt and run the machine until the dough comes together and forms a ball, pulling away from the sides of the processor bowl.

Remove the inner blade and scrape any excess dough into the bowl. Fold the chocolate chips into the dough using a spatula.

Using a 1-tablespoon cookie scoop, portion the dough into your hands. Roll into balls and place them at least 2 inches apart on the prepared baking sheet. You will need to do this in at least 2 batches depending on how large your baking sheet is. If you have 2 large baking sheets, you can portion all the dough onto the sheets and place one sheet in the fridge while you bake the other sheet. Alternatively, portion out the dough onto one sheet and place the remaining dough in the fridge while the first batch bakes.

Bake one sheet at a time on the middle rack for 18 to 20 minutes, until the edges are golden. Set the sheet on a wire rack to cool for 10 to 15 minutes before transferring the cookies to the rack with a spatula. Store in a container at room temperature or freeze for longer storage.

HOT TIPS "Partially softened" butter means softer than right out of the fridge but still with a chill to it. Let the vegan butter sticks sit on the counter in a bowl or the bowl of your stand mixer for about 20 minutes before creaming. That time varies depending on the type of climate you're in!

If there's a bit of cinnamon sugar left, keep it! You can sprinkle it on the **No-Churn Salted Caramel Tahini Ice Cream (page 226)** or make ice cream sandwiches with that recipe and these cookies, then sprinkle the cinnamon sugar on the sides.

SNICKLEDOODLES

26 mins.   56 mins.

TOPPING

3	tablespoons granulated sugar
1	tablespoon ground cinnamon

COOKIE DOUGH

1	tablespoon golden flax meal
3	tablespoons water
2½	cups all-purpose flour
1	teaspoon cream of tartar
1	teaspoon sea salt
½	teaspoon baking soda
1	cup (2 sticks) vegan butter, partially softened (see hot tips)
1½	cups granulated sugar
1	tablespoon vanilla extract

MAKES 33 COOKIES I didn't intend or even want to make snickerdoodles until I realized I could call them *snickledoodles*, after my cat, Snickles, and then it was as right as anything else in the universe. So they're now rebranded from this moment on. They're totally my cat's colors, after all, and just as sweet. Sorry you can't snuggle up to the real thing, but you can pretend while you eat a whole plate of these cookies and stare at this photo. For all cat lovers out there, make sure you follow @snicklesays on Instagram!

Preheat the oven to 375°F. Line a baking sheet with a Silpat mat or parchment paper.

To make the topping, combine the sugar and cinnamon in a bowl and set aside.

To make the dough, combine the flax meal and water in a small bowl and set aside to thicken. In another bowl, whisk together the flour, cream of tartar, sea salt, and baking soda and set aside.

Using a hand mixer and another large mixing bowl or in a stand mixer, cream the vegan butter and sugar together, about 2 minutes on medium to medium-high speed, until fluffy. Add the vanilla and the thickened flax meal mixture and continue to mix until well combined and fluffy.

Add the dry ingredients in 2 portions while mixing on low. (If using a hand mixer, I partially mix in the dry ingredients and then do the rest by hand with a spatula.) Mix until the dough is well combined and comes away from the sides of the bowl.

Using a 1½-tablespoon cookie scoop, portion the dough into your hands. Roll into a ball, coat in the cinnamon sugar topping, and slightly roll again if it has misshapen. Place the balls on the prepared baking sheet spaced 2 inches apart. I bake the cookies 8 per sheet, one sheet at a time, on the middle rack. The dough should still feel chilled when you make the balls. If not, be sure to refrigerate the portioned cookies before baking and refrigerate the dough between batches.

Bake for 14 minutes until golden. The cookies will be slightly puffy. Place the baking sheet on a wire rack. Let them rest for a few minutes and they will settle into a perfect crinkly cookie about 3 inches wide. Transfer the cookies to the wire rack to cool completely.

HOT TIP If you don't want to make all the cookies at once, freeze the unportioned dough. Thaw in the fridge overnight, then portion the dough, roll in cinnamon sugar, and bake as instructed.

COCONUT PECAN BISCOTTI

20 mins   70 mins.

C 40 mins. cooling

INGREDIENTS

1	tablespoon golden flax meal
3	tablespoons water
1	cup fine almond flour
1	cup gluten-free all-purpose flour
1½	teaspoons baking powder
½	teaspoon ground cinnamon
½	teaspoon sea salt
½	cup (1 stick) vegan butter, partially softened (see hot tips, page 208)
¼	cup granulated sugar
¼	cup packed light brown sugar
2	teaspoons vanilla extract
1	bar (4 oz/113 g) dairy-free semisweet baking chocolate, broken into squares, or ¾ cup vegan chocolate chips
⅓	cup finely chopped pecans
⅓	cup unsweetened shredded coconut

MAKES 10 BISCOTTI I'm so proud of myself for nailing a vegan and gluten-free biscotti that's light, crisp, and buttery and won't break your teeth. It's my ideal companion for coffee but it'll make teatime more fun, too! I dipped the bottoms in chocolate because this is how I remember biscotti from my local coffee shops, but you could drizzle it on top if you want less of it. And if you want to start experimenting with different flavor variations, you could easily swap the cinnamon for other spices like cardamom, ginger, or allspice; fold in dried currants, blueberries, or nuts other than pecans; and try other dry additions such as lemon or orange zest.

Preheat the oven to 350°F. Line a baking sheet with parchment paper.

In a small bowl, combine the flax meal and water and set aside to thicken.

In a mixing bowl, combine the almond flour, all-purpose flour, baking powder, cinnamon, and sea salt.

Using a hand mixer and another large mixing bowl or in a stand mixer, cream together the butter, granulated sugar, and brown sugar until fluffy, about 2 minutes. Add the thickened flax mixture and vanilla and continue to mix until combined. On low speed, gradually add the flour mixture until combined. Once the dough comes together, use a spatula to mix in the coconut and pecans until well combined.

Place the dough on the prepared baking sheet. Using your hands, form a rectangle ¾ inch thick and 9 to 10 inches by 4 inches.

Bake for 35 minutes, until the edges are golden brown and the cookie is slightly raised. Place the baking sheet on a wire rack and let the cookie cool for 35 to 40 minutes. You want to slice it while it's still a little warm and not completely cooled. Slice with a long, sharp knife on a slight diagonal every ¾ inch into 10 biscotti.

Gently place the biscotti on the parchment cut-side-down. Bake again for 30 to 35 minutes, flipping gently to the other cut side halfway through baking, until the cookies are firm to the touch and golden brown all over. Remove the baking sheet to a wire rack and let the biscotti cool completely before dipping in chocolate.

To melt the chocolate, place a heat-safe bowl over a pot with 1 or 2 inches of low simmering water. Melt the chocolate until smooth, or you can melt it in the microwave until smooth. Pour the melted chocolate into a wide shallow dish so you can dip the bottoms o the biscotti. Coat the bottoms and let the excess drip off, then lay them top-side-down on a wire rack. Decorate with chopped pecans or shredded coconut and allow to dry completely. Store in a container at room temperature or in the fridge.

DOUGHNUT HOLES 3 WAYS

⬦ 20 mins. ♨ 20 mins.

DOUGHNUTS

3–4	cups neutral vegetable oil, for frying
1	tablespoon golden flax meal
3	tablespoons water
½	cup soy milk
1	teaspoon apple cider vinegar
2	cups cake flour, plus more for dusting and rolling
½	cup granulated sugar
1½	teaspoons baking powder
½	teaspoon sea salt
⅛	teaspoon ground nutmeg
2	tablespoons melted vegan butter
2	teaspoons vanilla extract

TOPPINGS

For churro doughnut holes:
3 tablespoons granulated sugar combined with 1 teaspoon ground cinnamon

For coconut snowball doughnut holes: ½ cup shredded unsweetened coconut

For funfetti doughnut holes: ¼ cup vegan-friendly rainbow sprinkles

VANILLA GLAZE

2	cups confectioners' sugar, sifted
3–4	tablespoons nondairy milk
1	teaspoon vanilla extract

HOT TIP I find that organic confectioners' sugar needs to be sifted to make it powdery, without lumps. If using regular confectioners' sugar you can probably skip the sifting.

MAKES 24 TO 26 DOUGHNUT HOLES Doughnut holes are a fun way to enjoy fried dough in a portion-controlled way! I'm not usually about portion control, but when it comes to doughnuts, I have to watch it! They're my weakness. I have such fond memories of doughnut holes since I come from the country that invented them… Canada. Ever heard of a Timbit, eh? ANY occasion from the age of 3 to 23 called for Timbits, so the nostalgia is through the roof here. Get in on the fun and make them your fave way or all three ways I've suggested in this recipe. The more variety to choose from, the better!

Heat the fryer oil to 350 to 355°F in a deep fryer. If you're not using a deep fryer, then ensure that there's 2 to 3 inches of oil in a heavy-bottom pot or Dutch oven. Attach a thermometer to the side of the pot to monitor the oil temperature.

In a small bowl, combine the flax meal and water and set aside to thicken.

In another bowl, combine the nondairy milk with the apple cider vinegar and set aside to thicken and curdle.

In a large mixing bowl, whisk together the flour, sugar, baking powder, sea salt, and nutmeg.

Add the melted vegan butter, vanilla, and the thickened flax mixture to the nondairy milk mixture. Whisk together to combine well.

Create a well in the middle of the dry ingredients and pour the liquid ingredients into the well. Fold with a spatula until it comes together into a sticky ball of dough with no flour visible.

If you are making the churro doughnut holes, mix the sugar and cinnamon together in a small dish and set aside before you start deep frying. You'll need to coat the holes in the cinnamon sugar almost immediately out of the fryer so that it sticks. Otherwise, for glazed doughnut holes that you'll add coconut or sprinkles to, you can let them cool before glazing.

Cover a baking sheet with a wire rack and have ready another baking sheet or large plate lightly covered in flour. Lightly flour your hands and ideally using a cookie scoop, portion out 1 tablespoon of dough. Roll into a smooth ball in your palms. Place on the floured baking sheet or plate to prevent them from sticking. You can roll

all the doughnuts into balls and then fry them in batches. Fry in batches of about 6 at a time until golden brown, 3 to 4 minutes, rotating in the oil to get all sides evenly golden. Using tongs, transfer to the wire rack.

To make the vanilla glaze, combine the confectioners' sugar, nondairy milk, and vanilla in a mixing bowl. It should be a runny consistency that drips easily. Use your hand to coat each doughnut hole in the glaze, allowing the excess to drip off before coating in either shredded coconut or sprinkles while it's still wet. Place the doughnut hole back on the wire rack to dry completely.

Doughnut holes are always freshest and best eaten the day they're made!

LOAF CAKES 3 WAYS

All the loaf cake recipes can alternatively be made in a square 8 by 8-inch baking pan or divided into a 12-cup muffin pan. If making muffins, the bake time will be reduced to 35 to 45 minutes, until a toothpick comes out clean from the center.

LEMON CHIA SEED LOAF CAKE

 20 mins. 65 mins.

MAKES 1 LOAF (8 SLICES) This lemony loaf is chock-full of healthy chia seeds (good for digestion!) because I felt like giving a twist to the classic lemon poppy seed loaf. But if poppy seeds are what you have or what you prefer, by all means go for it. The cake will give you that perfect lemon tang you're looking for, and the glaze on top *IS* the icing on the cake that gives it a nice, sweet finishing touch.

BATTER

1	tablespoon golden flax meal
3	tablespoons water
2½	cups all-purpose flour
1½	teaspoons baking powder
½	teaspoon sea salt
¼	teaspoon baking soda
1	cup canned full-fat coconut milk
¾	cup granulated sugar
⅓	cup melted coconut oil
⅓	cup lemon juice (about 3 lemons)
2	tablespoons lemon zest (about 3 lemons)
2	teaspoons vanilla extract
2	tablespoons black chia seeds

LEMON GLAZE

1	cup confectioners' sugar, sifted
1½	tablespoons lemon juice (about half a lemon)
½	teaspoon lemon zest (about half a lemon)
½	teaspoon black chia seeds, for garnish

Preheat the oven to 350°F.

Use an 8 by 4-inch metal loaf pan. Cut a strip of parchment paper as wide as the length of the loaf pan so you can line it and have some overhang to lift the finished loaf out.

To make the batter, in a small bowl, combine the flax meal and water and set aside to thicken.

In a large mixing bowl, combine the flour, baking powder, sea salt, and baking soda and set aside.

In another bowl, whisk together the coconut milk, granulated sugar, coconut oil, lemon juice, lemon zest, and vanilla until smooth. Add this mixture to the dry ingredients along with the chia seeds and fold with a spatula until just combined and the batter has come away from the sides of the bowl.

Portion into the loaf pan and even out with a spatula on top and out to the edges, filling the pan. Bake for 60 to 65 minutes, until the edges are light golden brown and have come away from the sides, the top looks set and has slightly cracked, and a toothpick comes out clean from the center.

Place the pan on a wire rack to cool for 15 to 20 minutes. Lift the parchment paper to remove the cake, and place on the rack. Let the cake cool completely before icing.

To make the glaze, in a mixing bowl, combine the confectioners' sugar, lemon juice, and lemon zest until a smooth, runny consistency is created. You may need to add a tiny amount of water to get the right consistency. Only add ¼ teaspoon at a time until it's able to coat but drips easily off a spatula.

Place the cooled cake on a wire rack over a baking sheet. Pour the glaze on top of the loaf from one end to the other, generously coating the top, and use a spatula to spread it so that it completely covers the top of the loaf and spills over the edges, allowing the excess to drip down the sides. Sprinkle with the chia seeds and let it set before slicing and serving.

LOAF CAKES 3 WAYS

Continued

BLACK FOREST LOAF CAKE

 20 mins. 70 mins.

BATTER

1	tablespoon golden flax meal
3	tablespoons water
2	cups all-purpose flour
½	cup Dutch-processed cocoa powder, sifted
1½	teaspoons baking powder
½	teaspoon sea salt
¼	teaspoon baking soda
⅓	cup vegan butter
1	cup vegan chocolate chips or coarsely chopped dairy-free semisweet baking chocolate
½	cup granulated sugar
⅓	cup nondairy milk
2	teaspoons vanilla extract
1½	cups fresh or thawed frozen pitted whole cherries, cut in half

TOPPING

1	cup store-bought coconut whipped topping
½	cup fresh or thawed frozen pitted whole cherries
	Shaved or grated chocolate, for garnish (optional)

MAKES 1 LOAF (8 SLICES) I'm pretty sure the Black Forest cake I ate as a kid from the grocery store bakery was full of artificial cherry flavor as well as nasty maraschino cherries. No kirsch liqueur in sight! So I figured I'd try my hand at a real one. Seeing as I lived without kirsch all those years, I didn't think it was totally necessary to make you buy a liqueur you'll only use a few times, so I opted out. This is still rich and chocolatey and I've stuffed it with lots of actual cherries, which I think is REALLY what Black Forest is going for. If you're making this in cherry season, definitely go for fresh cherries all the way, and if you have kirsch in your cupboard, by all means soak your cherry garnish in a splash. If opting for frozen cherries, try finding sour cherries because they'd be even better than the dark sweet ones. Thaw frozen cherries completely, saving the juice for the finished loaf.

Preheat the oven to 350°F.

Use an 8 by 4-inch metal loaf pan. Cut a strip of parchment paper as wide as the length of the loaf pan so you can line it and have some overhang to lift the finished loaf out.

To make the batter, in a small bowl, combine the flax meal and water and set aside to thicken.

In a large mixing bowl, whisk together the flour, cocoa powder, baking powder, sea salt, and baking soda and set aside.

In a saucepan over medium-low heat, melt the butter. Turn the heat to low, add the chocolate, and stir constantly until melted and smooth. Remove the saucepan from the heat and stir in the sugar, nondairy milk, vanilla, and thickened flax mixture. Pour this mixture into the dry ingredients and add the cherries. Fold with a spatula until just combined and the batter has come away from the sides of the bowl.

Portion into the loaf pan and even out with a spatula on top and out to the edges, filling the pan. Bake for 60 to 65 minutes, until the edges have come away from the sides, the top looks set and is slightly cracked, and a toothpick comes out clean from the center.

Place the pan on a wire rack to cool for 15 to 20 minutes. Lift the parchment paper to remove the cake, and place on the rack. Let the cake cool completely before icing.

Take a skewer or toothpick and poke lots of holes all over the top about halfway down into the loaf. Spoon the reserved cherry juice, if you have it, over top. If you used fresh cherries, skip this step. It won't make or break the cake!

Top with coconut whipped topping, cherries, and shaved chocolate. Or you can serve the toppings with each slice of the cake.

LOAF CAKES 3 WAYS

Continued

PUMPKIN LOAF CAKE

 20 mins. 65 mins.

MAKES 1 LOAF (8 SLICES) You don't have to save this pumpkin cake for fall colors or winter weather! It's cozy all year round when you crave pumpkiny stuff and warm fragrant spices. Skip the icing and you have a great breakfast slice warmed up with some vegan butter, or give it that scrumptious layer of cream cheese frosting for those afternoons you need a sweet snack to get through the day.

BATTER

1	tablespoon golden flax meal
3	tablespoons water
2½	cups all-purpose flour
1½	teaspoons ground cinnamon
1½	teaspoons baking powder
1	teaspoon ground ginger
1	teaspoon ground nutmeg
1	teaspoon ground allspice
½	teaspoon ground cloves
½	teaspoon sea salt
¼	teaspoon baking soda
1	cup canned pure pumpkin puree
⅔	cup packed light brown sugar
⅓	cup melted vegan butter
2	tablespoons maple syrup
2	teaspoons vanilla extract
½	cup coarsely chopped pecans

CREAM CHEESE FROSTING

1½	cups confectioners' sugar, sifted
⅓	cup store-bought plain vegan cream cheese
1	teaspoon vanilla extract
1	teaspoon nondairy milk
¼	cup finely chopped pecans, for garnish

Preheat the oven to 350°F.

Use an 8 by 4-inch metal loaf pan. Cut a strip of parchment paper as wide as the length of the loaf pan so you can line it and have some overhang to lift the finished loaf out.

To make the batter, in a small bowl, combine the flax meal and water and set aside to thicken.

In a large mixing bowl, combine the flour, cinnamon, baking powder, ginger, nutmeg, allspice, cloves, sea salt, and baking soda and set aside.

In another bowl, whisk together the pumpkin puree, brown sugar, melted butter, maple syrup, vanilla, and the thickened flax mixture until smooth. Add this mixture to the dry ingredients along with the chopped pecans and fold with a spatula until just combined and the batter has come away from the sides of the bowl.

Portion into the loaf pan and even out with a spatula on top and out to the edges, filling the pan. Bake for 60 to 65 minutes, until the edges are light golden brown and have come away from the sides, the top looks set and is slightly cracked, and a toothpick comes out clean from the center.

Place the pan on a wire rack to cool for 15 to 20 minutes. Lift the parchment paper to remove the cake, and place on the rack. Let the cake cool completely before icing.

To make the cream cheese frosting, in a mixing bowl, combine the confectioners' sugar, cream cheese, vanilla, and nondairy milk in a mixing bowl with a spatula or a hand mixer until smooth.

Ice the top of the loaf using an offset spatula and top with the chopped pecans. Let it set before slicing.

stuff I eat...on a cozy sunday

These are the days I look forward to and dream of. I don't get a lot of them, but when I do, I make them count! Of course, I still make food because I can't *not*. But on these cozy Sundays, I actually want to do it as a form of self-care. When it's not about work, I get to eat what I crave, not what's within arm's reach or has to get eaten from testing. In addition to carbs, my off-day also includes binge watching, cuddles with Snickles, baking, and no Instagram, with a fave podcast and a bath to cap it off!

BRUNCH

homemade latte with maple syrup

some kind of fruit

chocolate almond crescent rolls
(page 235)

SNACK

old bay popcorn (page 182)

DINNER

one pot mac n' cheese (page 110)
with broccoli and peas thrown in

DESSERT

pumpkin loaf cake (page 219)

CHOCOLATE PEANUT BUTTER KRISPIE CAKE

10 mins. | 15 mins.

4 hrs. refrigeration

INGREDIENTS

½	cup vegan butter
2	cups all-natural smooth peanut butter
¾	cup maple syrup
1	teaspoon vanilla extract
1	teaspoon ground cinnamon
1	teaspoon sea salt
5	cups toasted brown rice cereal
3	bars (12 oz/339 g total) dairy-free semisweet baking chocolate, broken into squares, or 2 cups vegan chocolate chips
1	tablespoon coconut oil
¼	cup roasted salted peanuts, coarsely chopped

MAKES ONE 9-INCH CAKE (12 SLICES) Melting vegan marshmallows isn't a fun task, so I figured out how to make a yummy Rice Krispies Treat–style dessert without them. This recipe is inspired by something I get at a bakery in Toronto called Mabel's. I refer to their gooey yet crunchy slab of peanut butter and chocolate as "better than sex" because there's NOTHING better than this dessert. I'm not going to lie—I couldn't get mine to turn out exactly like their version, and sometimes secrets are best left in the vault. My version is still crazy good and left me satisfied, so I think you'll be turned on, too.

Line the bottom of a 9-inch springform pan with a large square of parchment paper so that there's some overhang. You can trim the excess if necessary, but it doesn't need to be neat. This is just so you can lift the finished cake onto a platter or cake stand.

In a large stockpot or Dutch oven over medium-low heat, add the vegan butter and allow it to melt completely. Once it's bubbling, reduce the heat to low and let the butter brown for about 4 minutes. Add the peanut butter, maple syrup, vanilla, cinnamon, and sea salt and stir until completely smooth and combined. Remove from the heat and fold in the cereal until well combined. Pour this into the springform pan and even it out while gently pressing the mixture down and all the way to the edges with a spatula.

To melt the chocolate, place a heat-safe bowl over a pot with 1 or 2 inches of low simmering water. Place the chocolate and coconut oil in the bowl and stir occasionally with a spatula until melted and smooth. Pour over the cake and gently shake the pan back and forth to get the chocolate spread out into an even layer all the way to the edges. Place the crushed peanuts on top and refrigerate for 2 to 4 hours.

Serve the cake partially chilled. Let it sit for about 20 minutes out of the fridge before slicing into wedges and serving.

Store the cake in the fridge and let it sit out at room temperature before eating so it's not too hard.

PASSION FRUIT SLICE

35 mins.　　10 mins.

C　minimum 3 hrs. refrigeration

NO-BAKE GRAHAM CRUST

9　sheets (18 squares) vegan graham crackers

½　teaspoon sea salt

⅓　cup melted vegan butter

PASSION FRUIT CURD

½　cup water

1　tablespoon agar flakes or 1 teaspoon agar powder

1¼　cups canned coconut cream (some liquid is fine)

1　cup passion fruit, including seeds (7 or 8 passion fruits)

¼　cup granulated sugar

TOPPINGS

Store-bought coconut whipped topping

Mint leaves, for garnish

MAKES ONE 9½-INCH PIE (12 SLICES) If you've ever seen me freak out about passion fruit anything on the Internet, you know the obsession is real. This rare and expensive tropical fruit is in the upper echelon of fruits. It's sour, sweet, fragrant, and just magical. I'm satisfied just smelling them over and over… and you know how much I like to smell things! I had to check a passion fruit dessert off my wish list. This slice of heaven is it, and it puts the fruit at the forefront. No passion fruit, no problem. Swapping passion fruit for something like mango or even dragon fruit would be cool (you can buy them in the frozen aisle!). If using one of those swaps, I would add some lime or lemon juice to tart it up.

To make the crust, in a food processor, pulse the graham crackers and sea salt into a fine crumb. Add the melted butter and pulse again until it comes together and looks like wet sand. Press evenly into a 9½-inch fluted pie pan. You will have enough to go at least three-quarters of the way up the sides of the pan. Refrigerate the crust while you make the rest of the recipe.

To make the curd, in a small saucepan over medium-low heat, whisk together the water and agar. Simmer for 5 to 6 minutes, until dissolved. You shouldn't see any flecks of agar in the liquid if using flakes, and the liquid will have reduced and thickened slightly.

At the same time, in a large saucepan over medium heat, whisk together the coconut cream, passion fruit, and sugar constantly for 2 to 3 minutes, until it just starts to bubble and is warmed through. Add the dissolved agar to this and whisk until well combined, about another 2 minutes. Transfer the mixture to a heat-safe glass bowl. Whisk it constantly to cool it down and prevent it from setting too much. It cannot be added to your chilled crust until it's tepid in temperature. Constantly stirring will help cool it quicker and prevent the agar from setting.

Once the mixture has cooled to about room temperature and with no steam present, pour it into the crust and refrigerate for at least 3 hours, until chilled and set.

To serve, top with a pile of the coconut whipped topping and garnish with the mint leaves. This is best eaten on the day it's made. I would consume it within 2 days max, otherwise the crust gets a little soggy.

NO-CHURN SALTED CARAMEL TAHINI ICE CREAM

20 mins.   8 mins.

minimum 6–7 hrs. in the freezer

ICE CREAM BASE

2   cans (13.5 oz/400 ml each) coconut cream (about 2⅛ cups total of thick cream, no liquid)

1   can (11.25 oz/320 g) sweetened condensed coconut milk (about 1 cup)

½   cup tahini, divided

3   frozen peeled bananas (best if only just ripe)

SALTED CARAMEL (MAKES JUST OVER ½ CUP)

1   cup coconut sugar

¼   cup unsweetened nondairy milk

3   tablespoons vegan butter

¾   teaspoon sea salt

MAKES ABOUT 8 SERVINGS (2 SMALL SCOOPS PER SERVING) This is a quick and easy recipe for making a creamy dreamy ice cream without an ice cream maker. Tahini is one of my fave pantry staples. It's inexpensive and nutritious and totally works in sweet stuff. I use it to make an easy glaze for sweet scones (page 31), and it's so good swirled into this ice cream with salted caramel. Some preparation is required in advance of making this. Remember to freeze the bananas and keep some cans of coconut cream in your fridge a few days ahead of making this, as you only want to use the thick cold cream without any liquid in it for the base. Oh, and throw a metal loaf pan in the freezer as well!

Freeze an 8 by 4-inch or 9 by 5-inch loaf pan for at least 2 hours before preparing the ice cream.

To make the ice cream base, to a high-powered blender add only the thick part of the coconut cream. (Reserve any residual coconut water or liquid milk for another use, or you can use it in the salted caramel in place of or mixed into the total amount of nondairy milk required.) Add the sweetened condensed coconut milk, ¼ cup of the tahini, and the frozen bananas and blend until very smooth. The mixture will be thick, so you might need to use the baton while blending or stop the blender to mix with a spatula a couple of times. Place this in the fridge while you make the salted caramel.

To make the salted caramel, to a small saucepan over medium-high heat, add the coconut sugar, nondairy milk, vegan butter, and sea salt and bring to a simmer, whisking constantly, 3 to 4 minutes. Once it's bubbling and foamy, rising in the saucepan, reduce the heat to medium low and continue whisking constantly for another 4 minutes or so, until it's thicker and can coat the side of the sauce-pan. On a thermometer it should be 220 to 230°F, or the thread stage. Let it stop bubbling and rest. You can also pour it into a heat-safe measuring cup so it's easy to pour and drizzle when assembling the ice cream in the loaf pan.

Do not line the loaf pan with parchment paper, as it just makes more of a mess when you're scooping the ice cream. Pour a quarter of the ice cream base into the pan. Shake the pan slightly to level

HOT TIP You could reserve a tablespoon of salted caramel to add to your glass for the **Salted Caramel Tahini Milkshake** (see photo on page 228).

the ice cream and fill it to all sides. Drizzle in a quarter of the caramel on the entire top surface. Then drizzle about 1 tablespoon of the remaining tahini. Add another layer of ice cream base and repeat with caramel and tahini ribbons. Repeat this twice more, finishing with caramel and tahini ribbons on the top.

Place the pan in the freezer. The best scooping texture is achieved after 6 to 7 hours; the time may vary, as every freezer is different. Once the ice cream has hardened, let it sit at room temperature anywhere from 15 to 25 minutes to soften a bit. Rinse your ice cream scoop under warm water before scooping.

Store in the freezer and cover with wrap to prevent freezer burn on the top. If you want to make the **Salted Caramel Tahini Milkshake (page 229)**, you'll need 2 large scoops or about 2 cups of ice cream per milkshake.

SALTED CARAMEL TAHINI MILKSHAKE

 5 mins.

use leftover No-Churn Salted Caramel Tahini Ice Cream (page 126)

2 cups No-Churn Salted Caramel Tahini Ice Cream

½ cup nondairy milk

1 tablespoon cacao nibs or dairy-free chocolate chips

1 tablespoon maple syrup

Store-bought coconut whipped topping, for garnish

Cacao nibs, dairy-free chocolate chips, or shaved chocolate, for garnish

MAKES 1 SHAKE The No-Churn Salted Caramel Tahini Ice Cream is rich, and I definitely only eat a small portion at a time. If you don't have anyone to help you eat it, you might be overwhelmed with having too much. But don't waste it! Even if it's turned into what looks like a bit of a mess and is frozen solid, that's a good sign that you should now blend it into this heavenly milkshake!

To a high-powered blender combine the ice cream, nondairy milk, cacao nibs or chocolate chips, and maple syrup and blend until smooth. Pour into your serving glass and top with the coconut whipped topping and cacao nibs.

PUMPKIN CHEESECAKE PINWHEELS

PUFF PASTRY 4 WAYS

I want to make you love puff pastry if you don't already. Since you can buy it already premade and frozen, using it is a good trick for making yourself look like a pro baker. So if you're getting the itch to make my puff pastry delights, make sure you thaw frozen store-bought puff pastry in the fridge overnight. Puff pastry comes in packages of two prerolled sheets, one prerolled, or one thicker hunk, more or less, that you need to roll thinner. You will be able to follow these recipes no matter what you find in your package.

STONE FRUIT GALETTE

CHOCOLATE ALMOND CRESCENT ROLLS

HOT PUFF PASTRY TIPS:

- Puff pastry is best eaten the day it's baked! But these goodies can be reheated in the oven for a few minutes at 425°F—if you even have leftovers!

- You have to work quickly, as the pastry can't get too warm. Whether it feels warm or not, always chill your shaped pastry in the fridge or freezer before baking. It should be cold going into the oven.

- If you have scraps from cutting out shapes, don't waste 'em! Bake these bits on their own and have fun twisting and shaping them any way your heart desires. Brush them with melted vegan butter and sprinkle cinnamon sugar or vegan cheese on them. Get creative!

- You can refreeze any unused puff pastry if it's been in the fridge for one day.

MINI STRAWBERRY TARTS

PUFF PASTRY 4 WAYS

Continued

INGREDIENTS

½ cup store-bought plain vegan cream cheese

½ cup canned pure pumpkin puree

¼ cup packed light brown sugar

¾ teaspoon ground cinnamon

¼ teaspoon ground ginger

All-purpose flour, for dusting

1 package (1 lb/500 g) frozen vegan puff pastry, thawed in the fridge

2 tablespoons melted vegan butter

2 tablespoons demerara sugar

PUMPKIN CHEESECAKE PINWHEELS

 20 mins.  C 2 hrs. freezing   20 mins.

MAKES 30 TO 34 PINWHEELS

In a mixing bowl, combine the vegan cream cheese, pumpkin puree, brown sugar, cinnamon, and ginger.

If the puff pastry is not already prerollled to about ⅛ inch thick, on a lightly floured surface, roll out the puff pastry with a rolling pin. If you have 1 sheet of pastry, roll it out to a large rectangle about 19 by 12 inches and ⅛ inch thick and spread all the filling out to the edges in an even layer. If you have 2 sheets, roll each sheet out to a rectangle about 14 by 10 inches and ⅛ inch thick, then divide the filling between each sheet and spread the mixture out in the same way. Roll the pastry up tightly from the shortest end. If you have 1 long log, cut it in half. Wrap the rolls in wax paper or plastic wrap and place in the freezer until much firmer and nearly frozen solid, 1 to 2 hours.

Preheat the oven to 450°F. Line a large baking sheet with a Silpat mat or parchment paper.

Once the rolls are chilled and firm so that filling won't leak out when slicing, take a long, sharp knife and cut ½-inch slices along the log. Do not press down but saw back and forth gently. Place the slices flat on the prepared baking sheet, spaced 1 to 2 inches apart. If they're slightly misshapen, you can reshape as best you can, but they will round out while baking. Brush the tops with melted butter and sprinkle with a pinch of demerara sugar.

Bake for 18 to 20 minutes, until golden brown and poufed. Place the pinwheels on a wire rack to cool. Repeat with the second batch.

MINI STRAWBERRY TARTS

20 mins.   20 mins.

MAKES 12 TARTS

INGREDIENTS

2   cups finely diced fresh strawberries
     (about 12 strawberries or half a pint)

1   tablespoon granulated sugar

1   teaspoon cornstarch

     All-purpose flour, for dusting

1   package (1 lb/500 g) frozen vegan
     puff pastry, thawed in the fridge

     Store-bought coconut whipped
     topping or vegan vanilla ice cream,
     for serving

Preheat the oven to 450°F.

In a mixing bowl, combine the strawberries, sugar, and cornstarch and set aside.

If the puff pastry is not already prerolled to about ⅛ inch thick, on a lightly floured surface, roll out the puff pastry with a rolling pin. Use a 3 to 3½-inch cookie cutter to punch 12 rounds. Don't twist the cookie cutter or it'll reduce how high the puff pastry will rise.

Transfer each round to a 12-cup muffin pan and gently press each round into the bottom of a muffin cup. Use a fork to prick holes only into the center of the rounds, being careful not to prick the edges. You want the edges to rise around the filling.

Fill each pastry cup with a heaping tablespoon of the strawberry mixture. Bake for 18 to 20 minutes, until the pastry has risen and is slightly golden. Let cool for 10 minutes, then use a small knife or offset spatula to nudge the tarts out of the muffin pan onto a wire rack. Serve either slightly warm or completely cooled and top with coconut whipped topping or vegan vanilla ice cream.

PUFF PASTRY 4 WAYS

Continued

STONE FRUIT GALETTE

 20 mins.   20 mins.

MAKES 8 SLICES

ALMOND FILLING

¾	cup fine almond flour
½	cup packed light brown sugar
⅓	cup melted vegan butter
1	teaspoon ground cinnamon

GALETTE

2	cups thinly sliced peaches, skin on (2 peaches)
1	cup thinly sliced plums, skin on (2 plums)
2	tablespoons lemon juice (about 1 lemon)
	All-purpose flour, for dusting
1	package (1 lb/500 g) frozen vegan puff pastry, thawed in the fridge
1	tablespoon melted vegan butter
1	teaspoon demerara sugar

Preheat the oven to 450°F. Line a large baking sheet with a Silpat mat or parchment paper.

To make the almond filling, in a bowl, combine the almond flour, brown sugar, melted vegan butter, and cinnamon and set aside.

To make the galette, in another bowl, combine the sliced peaches and plums with the lemon juice and set aside.

On a lightly floured surface, roll out the puff pastry with a rolling pin. If you have 2 sheets of puff pastry, roll out one of the sheets to a 10 by 12-inch rectangle and transfer to the prepared baking sheet. If you have only 1 piece of puff pastry, then roll it out to double the size and then slice in half into 2 rectangles of equal size. Transfer one rectangle to the prepared baking sheet. Spread the almond filling in an even layer, leaving 1 inch clean from the edges.

Roll out the other puff pastry sheet to a 10 by 12-inch rectangle. Cut out a window from this rectangle 1 inch from the inside edges. You can reserve this inner piece for another use or make a cross-hatch pattern for the top, if desired.

Take ½ tablespoon of the melted butter and brush or dab it around the bare edge of the pastry on the baking sheet around the almond filling. Then place the border of pastry on top and gently press the 1-inch edge on top without making indents in the pastry.

Alternate slices of peaches and plums in 4 rows across the inner area. Brush the remaining melted butter on the border of pastry and then sprinkle with the demerara sugar.

Bake for 18 to 20 minutes, until the edges are puffed and golden brown. Leave the galette on the baking sheet and transfer to a wire rack to cool for 15 to 20 minutes before slicing and serving.

CHOCOLATE ALMOND CRESCENT ROLLS

 30 mins.   15–17 mins.

MAKES 8 ROLLS

Preheat the oven to 450°F. Line a baking sheet with a Silpat mat or parchment paper.

If you have 2 sheets of puff pastry, work with 1 sheet at a time and leave the other in the fridge. On a lightly floured surface, roll the pastry with a rolling pin into a rectangle that's about 12 by 8 inches wide. If you have 1 sheet, the rectangle will be about double the width, so 12 by 16 inches wide. Use a dough cutter or pizza cutter to trim the edges slightly to make them straight. Cut on a 45-degree angle from one bottom corner to the top edge and then from that point back down on a 45-degree angle. Do this all across your sheet so you have triangle shapes. They won't all be precisely even.

Add 1 tablespoon each of chocolate chips and sliced almonds near the wide end of the triangle. Fold the pastry over the filling and roll up tightly toward the point, while lightly pinching the ends and curving them slightly away from the direction you're rolling to seal in the filling. It should look like a crescent roll, and the tip of the triangle should be tucked under the bottom. If they're not all perfect in size, it's OK!

Place the crescent rolls slightly spaced apart on the baking sheet.

Brush the rolls with melted butter and place a few sliced almonds on top. Bake for 15 to 17 minutes, until golden brown. Transfer to a wire rack and let cool for at least 20 minutes. The filling will be extremely hot! Dust with confectioners' sugar before serving.

INGREDIENTS

All-purpose flour, for dusting

1 package (1 lb/500 g) frozen vegan puff pastry, thawed in the fridge

½ cup vegan chocolate chips

½ cup sliced almonds, plus more for garnish

1 tablespoon melted vegan butter

2 teaspoons confectioners' sugar, for garnish

stuff I eat...when I travel

I can't possibly include EVERYTHING I've eaten on my travels, so for more comprehensive lists and reviews, you can check out the travel section of hotforfoodblog.com or my vlogs on YouTube. But here are highlights for some of the bigger cities I've been to, and these are most definitely *hot for food*–approved!

CALGARY

The Coup

Hoopla Donuts

Ten Foot Henry *(order all the vegetable dishes that can be made vegan!)*

LAS VEGAS

Chef Kenny's Asian Vegan Restaurant

Ronald's Donuts

Tacotarian

Terrace Pointe Café at Wynn Las Vegas *(get the chicken and waffles)*

VegeNation

LOS ANGELES

Crossroads Kitchen *(fine dining)*

Donut Friend

The Good Good Vegan Kitchen + Bakeshop *(they have croissants!)*

Joy *(order the vegan dan dan noodles)*

Magpies Softserve

Tatsu *(order the hippie ramen)*

Veggie Grill, Buddy's, or Monty's Good Burger *(burgers and fast food)*

MONTREAL

ChuChai

Sophie Sucrée

NEW YORK & BROOKLYN

Dun-Well Doughnuts

Kajitsu *(upscale Japanese experience)*

Orchard Grocer

Screamer's Pizzeria

Very Fresh Noodles *(order the mock duck)*

PARIS

La Palanche d'Âulac

Mon Epicerie Paris *(vegan grocery store)*

VG Pâtisserie

SAN DIEGO

Donna Jean

Plant Power Fast Food

TORONTO

Copenhagen Vegan Café & Bakery

The Hogtown Vegan

Fat Choi/Soos

Fresh Restaurants

Through Being Cool Vegan Baking Co.

VANCOUVER

The Acorn Restaurant

The Arbor

Chau Veggie Express

To Die For Fine Foods

Kokomo

Virtuous Pie

about the author

LAUREN TOYOTA is the author of the best-selling cookbook *Vegan Comfort Classics: 101 Recipes to Feed Your Face*. She's been named one of Canada's Most Influential Vegans (*Impact Magazine*) and has appeared on many national television programs sharing her expertise for making vegan food fast and fun. Lauren's YouTube channel, Instagram, and blog, hot for food, have amassed millions of views and devoted fans.

www.hotforfoodblog.com

 @hotforfood / @laurentoyota

/ hotforfoodblog

acknowledgments

THANK YOU THE MOST! My followers are the reason I do what I do. Thank you for making the recipes, sharing the food, posting the pics, telling your friends and fam about hot for food, and sharing this cookbook with others.

Michelle Li, you are a kitchen wizard with great taste and a nose for good food. Thank you for helping develop recipes, testing, editing videos, planning, and in general keeping me organized!

Big thanks to Eugenia Zykova, who took the majority of the recipe shots and edited all the photography in the book. I'm so thankful for your help with this massive project. You are truly one-of-a-kind, and I appreciate your work ethic and vision.

Thank you, Vanessa Heins, for always making me look good while feeding my face, being up for anything, and making me laugh. You're so talented and just the best!

Thank you to Alex Dale and Olivia Brown for being on the team and being a massive help behind the scenes while I embarked on this cookbook project.

Thank you to my hardworking cooks in the recipe-testing group: Jasmine Bui, Bianca Migueles, Kendra Korinetz, Erin Yantha, Alexa Tucker, Samantha eetjen, Kristy LaPointe, Laura Takahashi, Jon Lubanksi, Lindsay Gruis Brown, and Amy Nowak.

Thank you to the publishing team—Kelly Snowden, Isabelle Gioffredi, Emma Rudolph, Dan Myers, Allison Renzulli, and Lauren Kretzschmar, Andrea Magyar, Abdi Omer, Michelle Arbus, and everyone who has had a hand in this at Ten Speed Press and Penguin Canada. Thank you for trusting me and letting me create!

Love to Timothy Pakron, who helped motivate and inspire me creatively during the making of this book!

Big love to Michael Cammidge and Snickles, who probably have the worst job of all—being my snuggle buddies, shoulders to cry on, and ears to vent to when I'm freaking out about creating and failing. Love you.

Gratitude and love to Tiffany Astle at penelopePR, Sally Ekus and the team at The Lisa Ekus Group, Ashley Riske, Aimée Legault, and the whole team at Kin Canada/Corus Entertainment. Thank you for ALL you do and the hours you dedicate to helping to grow my business.

—xo Lauren

index

A

Aioli, Gochujang, 191
almonds
    Chocolate Almond Crescent
        Rolls, 235
    Stone Fruit Galette, 234
apples
    Apple Crumble Muffins, 36
    Immune Warrior Juice, 41
    Real Green Juice, 41
    The "Sharp" Grilled Cheese, 104
artichokes
    Dill Pickle Popcorn Seasoning
        + Snack Mix, 181
    Fried Artichoke Sandwich, 70–71
avocados
    All-Green Fresh Rolls with Green
        Curry Dipping Sauce, 160
    Charred Corn Salad, 150
    Fries & Salad, 80
    Tortilla Soup, 46–47

B

bacon, vegan
    Bacon Kale Pasta, 127
    Beet Bacon, 66
    Tempeh Bacon Chunks, 100
    Zucchini Carbonara, 146–47
baking staples, 10
bananas
    My Fave Smoothie, 43
    No-Churn Salted Caramel Tahini
        Ice Cream, 226–27
bars
    Baked Peanut Butter & Jam Oat
        Bars, 35
    Rocky Road Bars, 205
beans
    Breakfast Totchos, 22–23
    canned, 8
    Crunchy Butter Beans, 96

    HFF Famous Bowls, 153
    Tex-Mex Mac n' Cheese, 119
    Tortilla Soup, 46–47
    Zuppa Toscana, 62–63
    See also mung beans
bean sprouts
    Thai Red Curry Mac n'
        Cheese, 116
beets
    Beet Bacon, 66
    Clubhouse Sandwich, 66–67
    Immune Warrior Juice, 41
    Pink Beet Caramel Popcorn, 183
    Pink Goddess Dressing, 200
binders, 4
Biscotti, Coconut Pecan, 210–11
Black Forest Loaf Cake, 216–17
blueberries
    Blueberry Lemon Scones, 30
    Pink Beet Caramel Popcorn
        + Snack Mix, 183
bok choy
    Kabocha Broth with Udon, 135
    Steamed Kale, Bok Choy &
        Broccoli, 89
bowls
    cooked vegetables for, 86–89
    grain bases for, 84–85
    hearty additions for, 90–100
    HFF Famous Bowls, 153
    making, 82–83
bread, 11
    Old Bay Croutons, 197
    See also sandwiches
Breakfast Totchos, 22–23
Breakfast Za, 20
broccoli
    Easy Tofu & Veggie Stir-Fry,
        128–29
    Steamed Kale, Bok Choy &
        Broccoli, 89

brussels sprouts
    Easy Brussels Sprouts Pasta,
        124–25
    My Everyday Roasted Vegetable
        Salad, 76–77
    Roasted Vegetables, 76
Buffalo Chicken Crunch Wraps,
    142–43
Buffalo Chicken Mac n' Cheese, 113
Burritos, Korean BBQ, 140–41
Butter Chicken Nachos, 158–59
Butter Chicken Sauce, 158–59

C

cabbage
    Blistered Shishito Peppers with
        Ramen, 168
    Cabbage Slaw, 70
    Charred Corn Salad, 150
    Easy Tofu & Veggie Stir-Fry,
        128–29
    Fried Artichoke Sandwich, 70–71
    Korean BBQ Burritos, 140–41
    My Everyday Roasted Vegetable
        Salad, 76–77
    Roasted Purple Cabbage Slaw, 88
    Roasted Vegetable Potstickers,
        78–79
    Spicy Lentil Wrap, 69
Cacio e Pepe, 58
Caesar Dressing, Tahini, 200
cakes
    Black Forest Loaf Cake, 216–17
    Chocolate Peanut Butter Krispie
        Cake, 222
    Lemon Chia Seed Loaf Cake,
        214–15
    Pumpkin Loaf Cake, 219
caramel
    No-Churn Salted Caramel Tahini
        Ice Cream, 226–27

Pink Beet Caramel Popcorn, 183
Salted Caramel, 226
Salted Caramel Tahini
    Milkshake, 229
cashews
    Cilantro Sour Cream, 189
    Corn Chowder, 56–57
    Everything Bagel Popcorn
        Seasoning + Snack Mix, 181
    Smoky Cheese Spread, 174
    Thai Red Curry Mac n'
        Cheese, 116
cauliflower
    Cauliflower Steaks with Spaghetti
        Aglio e Olio, 136–39
    My Everyday Roasted Vegetable
        Salad, 76–77
    Roasted Cauliflower Rice, 140–41
    Roasted Curry Cauliflower, 89
    Roasted Vegetables, 76
    The "Spiced" Grilled Cheese, 105
cheese, vegan, 5
    Bacon Kale Pasta, 127
    Breakfast Totchos, 22–23
    Breakfast Za, 20
    Buffalo Chicken Crunch Wraps,
        142–43
    Buffalo Chicken Mac n'
        Cheese, 113
    Butter Chicken Nachos, 158–59
    Cacio e Pepe, 58
    Cauliflower Steaks with Spaghetti
        Aglio e Olio, 136–39
    Chipotle Cheese Fries, 51
    Chipotle Cheese Sauce, 51
    Cream Cheese Frosting, 219
    Creamy Green Pea Soup with
        Pasta & Parmesan, 55
    The "Creamy" Grilled Cheese, 107
    Easy Brussels Sprouts Pasta,
        124–25
    Fries & Salad, 80
    Green Mac n' Cheese, 120
    Jalapeño Cheddar Scones, 30
    Kabocha Stuffed Shells, 130–31
    Kabocha Wonton Ravioli with
        Miso Butter, 132–33
    Korean BBQ Burritos, 140–41
    Mushroom Kimchi Omelet, 18
    My Everyday Sandwich, 75
    One-Pot Mac n' Cheese, 110

Pizza Mac n' Cheese, 114–15
Pumpkin Cheesecake
    Pinwheels, 232
Ragu Bolognese, 122–23
Red Sauce Enchiladas, 48–49
Savory Broken Scone Breakfast
    Muffins, 32
Savory Cheese Tart, 177
The "Sharp" Grilled Cheese, 104
Sloppy Joe Zucchini Boats, 145
Smoky Cheese Spread, 174
The "Spiced" Grilled Cheese, 105
Stuffed Breakfast Danishes, 24–25
Stuffed Potato Skins with Onion
    Dip, 164–65
Sweet & Sour Rice Balls, 186–87
The "Sweet" Grilled Cheese, 106
Tex-Mex Mac n' Cheese, 119
Thai Red Curry Mac n'
    Cheese, 116
Tofu Ricotta, 130
Warm Shishito Pepper Dip, 173
Zucchini Carbonara, 146–47
cherries
    Black Forest Loaf Cake, 216–17
chia seeds
    Crunchy Coconut Granola, 38–39
    Lemon Chia Seed Loaf Cake,
        214–15
chicken, vegan, 6
    Buffalo Chicken Crunch Wraps,
        142–43
    Buffalo Chicken Mac n'
        Cheese, 113
    Butter Chicken Nachos, 158–59
    Chicken Shawarma, 99
    Korean BBQ Burritos, 140–41
    Thai Red Curry Mac n'
        Cheese, 116
chipotle peppers
    Chipotle Cheese Fries, 51
    Chipotle Cheese Sauce, 51
    Red Sauce, 48
chocolate
    Black Forest Loaf Cake, 216–17
    Chocolate Almond Crescent
        Rolls, 235
    Chocolate Chip Corn Cookies, 206
    Chocolate Peanut Butter Krispie
        Cake, 222
    Coconut Pecan Biscotti, 210–11

Pink Beet Caramel Popcorn
    + Snack Mix, 183
Rocky Road Bars, 205
Salted Caramel Tahini
    Milkshake, 229
Chowder, Corn, 56–57
Churro Doughnut Holes, 212–13
Chutney, Mango, 105
Cilantro Sour Cream, 189
Citrus Juice, Sunny, 41
Clubhouse Sandwich, 66–67
coconut
    Coconut Pecan Biscotti, 210–11
    Coconut Snowball Doughnut
        Holes, 212–13
    cream and milk, 4
    Crunchy Coconut Granola, 38–39
coffee
    My Fave Smoothie, 43
condiments, 8–9
convenience products, vegan, 5–6, 11
cookies
    Chocolate Chip Corn
        Cookies, 206
    Coconut Pecan Biscotti, 210–11
    Snickledoodles, 208–9
corn
    Cacio e Pepe, 58
    Charred Corn Salad, 150
    Chocolate Chip Corn
        Cookies, 206
    Corn Chowder, 56–57
    Corn Chowder Hollandaise, 60
    HFF Famous Bowls, 153
    Kabocha Broth with Udon, 135
    Red Sauce Enchiladas, 48–49
    Tex-Mex Mac n' Cheese, 119
    Tortilla Soup, 46–47
    See also popcorn
Croutons, Old Bay, 197
currants
    My Everyday Roasted Vegetable
        Salad, 76–77
    Savory Cheese Tart, 177

D

dairy, vegan, 11
Danishes, Stuffed Breakfast, 24–25
deli meat, vegan, 5
    My Everyday Sandwich, 75
Dill Pickle Popcorn Seasoning, 181

dips
    Classic Onion Dip, 163
    Warm Shishito Pepper Dip, 173
Doughnut Holes, 212–13

E

Egg Yolk Sauce, 188
Enchiladas, Red Sauce, 48–49
equipment, 7
Everything Bagel Popcorn
    Seasoning, 181

F

fries
    Chipotle Cheese Fries, 51
    Fries & Salad, 80
    frozen, 6
    Tokyo Street Fries, 185
Frosting, Cream Cheese, 219
fruits
    dried, 10
    fresh, 7
    Stone Fruit Galette, 234
    Sunny Citrus Juice, 41
    See also individual fruits
Funfetti Doughnut Holes, 212–13

G

Galette, Stone Fruit, 234
glazes
    Lemon Glaze, 214–15
    Tahini Glaze, 31
    Vanilla Glaze, 212–13
Gochujang Aioli, 191
grains, 10
granola
    Crunchy Coconut Granola, 38–39
    Rocky Road Bars, 205
grapefruit
    Sunny Citrus Juice, 41
Gravy, Pumpkin Miso, 193
Green Curry Dipping Sauce, 160
greens
    Fries & Salad, 80
    Green Mac n' Cheese, 120
    Real Green Juice, 41
    See also individual greens
grilled cheese
    The "Creamy" Grilled Cheese, 107
    The "Sharp" Grilled Cheese, 104
    The "Spiced" Grilled Cheese, 105
    The "Sweet" Grilled Cheese, 106

ground round, veggie, 5
    Sloppy Joe Zucchini Boats, 145

H

herbs, 8
Hollandaise, Corn Chowder, 60
Hummus Dressing, Use Up the, 201

I

ice cream
    No-Churn Salted Caramel Tahini
        Ice Cream, 226–27
    Salted Caramel Tahini
        Milkshake, 229
Immune Warrior Juice, 41
ingredients, 3–11

J

jackfruit
    Tortilla Soup, 46–47
jalapeños
    Jalapeño Cheddar Scones, 30
    Jalapeño Ranch, 190
jam
    Baked Peanut Butter & Jam Oat
        Bars, 35
    The "Sweet" Grilled Cheese, 106
juices
    Immune Warrior Juice, 41
    My Blender Juice, 41
    Real Green Juice, 41
    Sunny Citrus Juice, 41

K

kabocha squash
    Kabocha Broth with Udon, 135
    Kabocha Stuffed Shells, 130–31
    Kabocha Wonton Ravioli with
        Miso Butter, 132–33
    Miso-Roasted Kabocha Squash,
        94–95
kala namak, 4–5
kale
    Bacon Kale Pasta, 127
    Breakfast Za, 20
    My Everyday Roasted Vegetable
        Salad, 76–77
    Real Green Juice, 41
    Steamed Kale, Bok Choy &
        Broccoli, 89
    Zuppa Toscana, 62–63

kimchi
    Korean BBQ Burritos, 140–41
    Mushroom Kimchi Omelet, 18
Korean BBQ Burritos, 140–41

L

lemons
    Blueberry Lemon Scones, 30
    Lemon Chia Seed Loaf Cake,
        214–15
    Lemon Glaze, 214–15
    Sunny Citrus Juice, 41
Lentil Wrap, Spicy, 69
lettuce
    All-Green Fresh Rolls with Green
        Curry Dipping Sauce, 160
    Buffalo Chicken Crunch Wraps,
        142–43
    Fries & Salad, 80
    Grilled Romaine Hearts, 88
limes
    Sunny Citrus Juice, 41

M

mac n' cheese
    Buffalo Chicken Mac n'
        Cheese, 113
    Green Mac n' Cheese, 120
    One-Pot Mac n' Cheese, 110
    Pizza Mac n' Cheese, 114–15
    Tex-Mex Mac n' Cheese, 119
    Thai Red Curry Mac n'
        Cheese, 116
Mango Chutney, 105
marshmallows
    Rocky Road Bars, 205
menus
    for busy times, 149
    for casual get-togethers, 64–65
    for cozy Sundays, 221
    everyday, 72
Milkshake, Salted Caramel Tahini, 229
miso
    Miso Butter Sauce, 132
    Miso-Roasted Kabocha Squash,
        94–95
    Pumpkin Miso Gravy, 193
muffins
    Apple Crumble Muffins, 36
    Savory Broken Scone Breakfast
        Muffins, 32

mung beans
Breakfast Totchos, 22–23
Breakfast Za, 20
Mung Bean Scramble, 17
Savory Broken Scone Breakfast
Muffins, 32
Stuffed Breakfast Danishes,
24–25
mushrooms
Kabocha Broth with Udon, 135
Mushroom Kimchi Omelet, 18
Mushroom Kraut Potato Cakes,
154–55
Ragu Bolognese, 122–23
Roasted Vegetable Potstickers,
78–79

N

Nachos, Butter Chicken, 158–59
nuts, 10. *See also individual nuts*

O

oats
Apple Crumble Muffins, 36
Baked Peanut Butter & Jam Oat
Bars, 35
Crunchy Coconut Granola, 38–39
oils, 3, 9
Old Bay Seasoning
Old Bay Croutons, 197
Old Bay Popcorn Seasoning, 182
olives
Bacon Kale Pasta, 127
Fries & Salad, 80
oil, 3
Sundried Tomato, Olive & Chive
Scones, 30
Omelet, Mushroom Kimchi, 18
onions
Caramelized Onions, 104
Classic Onion Dip, 163
Crispy Onion Strings, 194
oranges
Sunny Citrus Juice, 41

P

passion fruit
Passion Fruit Curd, 225
Passion Fruit Slice, 225
pasta and noodles, 10
Bacon Kale Pasta, 127

Blistered Shishito Peppers with
Ramen, 168
Cacio e Pepe, 58
Cauliflower Steaks with Spaghetti
Aglio e Olio, 136–39
Creamy Green Pea Soup with
Pasta & Parmesan, 55
Easy Brussels Sprouts Pasta,
124–25
Easy Tofu & Veggie Stir-Fry,
128–29
Kabocha Broth with Udon, 135
Kabocha Stuffed Shells, 130–31
Kabocha Wonton Ravioli with
Miso Butter, 132–33
Ragu Bolognese, 122–23
Zucchini Carbonara, 146–47
See also mac n' cheese
peaches
Stone Fruit Galette, 234
peanut butter
Baked Peanut Butter & Jam Oat
Bars, 35
Chocolate Peanut Butter Krispie
Cake, 222
Rocky Road Bars, 205
peanuts
Chocolate Peanut Butter Krispie
Cake, 222
Old Bay Popcorn Seasoning
+ Snack Mix, 182
Thai Red Curry Mac n'
Cheese, 116
peas
All-Green Fresh Rolls with Green
Curry Dipping Sauce, 160
Creamy Green Pea Soup, 52
Creamy Green Pea Soup with
Pasta & Parmesan, 55
Green Mac n' Cheese, 120
pecans
Coconut Pecan Biscotti, 210–11
Crunchy Coconut Granola, 38–39
Pumpkin Loaf Cake, 219
peppers
Easy Tofu & Veggie Stir-Fry,
128–29
Kabocha Stuffed Shells, 130–31
Korean BBQ Burritos, 140–41
Pizza Mac n' Cheese, 114–15

Roasted Red Pepper Sauce,
130–31
Sloppy Joe Zucchini Boats, 145
Spicy Lentil Wrap, 69
Tex-Mex Mac n' Cheese, 119
Tortilla Soup, 46–47
See also chipotle peppers;
jalapeños; shishito peppers
Pesto Dressing, Creamy, 201
pies
Passion Fruit Slice, 225
Pink Beet Caramel Popcorn + Snack
Mix, 183
Pink Goddess Dressing, 200
Pinwheels, Pumpkin
Cheesecake, 232
pistachios
Green Mac n' Cheese, 120
Pink Beet Caramel Popcorn
+ Snack Mix, 183
Savory Cheese Tart, 177
pizza
Breakfast Za, 20
Pizza Mac n' Cheese, 114–15
plums
Stone Fruit Galette, 234
popcorn
Dill Pickle Popcorn Seasoning
+ Snack Mix, 181
Everything Bagel Popcorn
Seasoning + Snack Mix, 181
Homemade Stove-Top
Popcorn, 180
Old Bay Popcorn Seasoning
+ Snack Mix, 182
Pink Beet Caramel Popcorn
+ Snack Mix, 183
tips for, 179
Tokyo Mix Popcorn Seasoning
+ Snack Mix, 182
poppy seeds
Everything Bagel Popcorn
Seasoning, 181
potatoes
Chipotle Cheese Fries, 51
Corn Chowder, 56–57
Creamy Mashed Potatoes, 153
Fries & Salad, 80
HFF Famous Bowls, 153
Mushroom Kraut Potato Cakes,
154–55

potatoes, *continued*
    Smoky Cheese Spread, 174
    Stuffed Potato Skins with Onion
        Dip, 164–65
    Tokyo Street Fries, 185
    Two Potato Rösti, 26
    Zuppa Toscana, 62–63
potlucks, 170
Potstickers, Roasted Vegetable,
    78–79
pretzels
    Old Bay Popcorn Seasoning
        + Snack Mix, 182
    Rocky Road Bars, 205
puff pastry
    Chocolate Almond Crescent
        Rolls, 235
    frozen vegan, 6, 230
    Mini Strawberry Tarts, 233
    Pumpkin Cheesecake
        Pinwheels, 232
    Stone Fruit Galette, 234
    Stuffed Breakfast Danishes, 24–25
    tips for, 231
pumpkin
    HFF Famous Bowls, 153
    Pumpkin Cheesecake
        Pinwheels, 232
    Pumpkin Loaf Cake, 219
    Pumpkin Miso Gravy, 193
pumpkin seeds
    Bacon Kale Pasta, 127
    My Everyday Roasted Vegetable
        Salad, 76–77
    Savory Cheese Tart, 177

R

Ragu Bolognese, 122–23
Ranch, Jalapeño, 190
Ravioli, Kabocha Wonton, with
    Miso Butter, 132–33
Red Sauce, 48
Red Sauce Enchiladas, 48–49
Rice Balls, Sweet & Sour, 186–87
rice cereal
    Chocolate Peanut Butter Krispie
        Cake, 222
Rocky Road Bars, 205
rolls
    All-Green Fresh Rolls with Green
        Curry Dipping Sauce, 160

Chocolate Almond Crescent
    Rolls, 235
Rösti, Two Potato, 26

S

salad dressings
    Creamy Pesto Dressing, 201
    Jalapeño Ranch, 190
    Pink Goddess Dressing, 200
    Sesame Soy Vinaigrette, 201
    Tahini Caesar Dressing, 200
    Use Up the Hummus
        Dressing, 201
salads
    Charred Corn Salad, 150
    Fries & Salad, 80
    My Everyday Roasted Vegetable
        Salad, 76–77
    See also slaws
sandwiches
    Clubhouse Sandwich, 66–67
    The "Creamy" Grilled Cheese, 107
    Fried Artichoke Sandwich, 70–71
    My Everyday Sandwich, 75
    The "Sharp" Grilled Cheese, 104
    The "Spiced" Grilled Cheese, 105
    The "Sweet" Grilled Cheese, 106
sauces
    Butter Chicken Sauce, 158–59
    Chipotle Cheese Sauce, 51
    Cilantro Sour Cream, 189
    Corn Chowder Hollandaise, 60
    Egg Yolk Sauce, 188
    Gochujang Aioli, 191
    Green Curry Dipping Sauce, 160
    Miso Butter Sauce, 132
    Ragu Bolognese, 122–23
    Red Sauce, 48
    Roasted Red Pepper Sauce,
        130–31
    Sesame Ginger Sauce, 192
    Sweet & Sour Sauce, 186–87
sauerkraut
    Mushroom Kraut Potato Cakes,
        154–55
    My Everyday Sandwich, 75
sausage, vegan
    Breakfast Za, 20
    Pizza Mac n' Cheese, 114–15
    Stuffed Breakfast Danishes,
        24–25
    Zuppa Toscana, 62–63

scones
    Blueberry Lemon Scones, 30
    Jalapeño Cheddar Scones, 30
    making, 28–30
    Savory Broken Scone Breakfast
        Muffins, 32
    Strawberry Cardamom
        Scones, 30
    Sundried Tomato, Olive & Chive
        Scones, 30
seasoning mixes
    Dill Pickle Popcorn Seasoning, 181
    Everything Bagel Popcorn
        Seasoning, 181
    Old Bay Popcorn Seasoning, 182
    storing, 178
    Tokyo Mix Popcorn
        Seasoning, 182
seeds, 10. *See also individual seeds*
sesame oil, 3
    Sesame Ginger Sauce, 192
    Sesame Soy Vinaigrette, 201
sesame seeds
    Everything Bagel Popcorn
        Seasoning, 181
Shawarma, Chicken, 99
shishito peppers
    Blistered Shishito Peppers,
        166–67
    Blistered Shishito Peppers with
        Ramen, 168
    Warm Shishito Pepper Dip, 173
slaws
    Cabbage Slaw, 70
    Roasted Purple Cabbage Slaw, 88
Sloppy Joe Zucchini Boats, 145
Smoothie, My Fave, 43
Snickledoodles, 208–9
soups
    Corn Chowder, 56–57
    Creamy Green Pea Soup, 52
    Creamy Green Pea Soup with
        Pasta & Parmesan, 55
    Kabocha Broth with Udon, 135
    Tortilla Soup, 46–47
    Zuppa Toscana, 62–63
Sour Cream, Cilantro, 189
soy curls, 6
    Buffalo Chicken Crunch Wraps,
        142–43
    Buffalo Chicken Mac n'
        Cheese, 113

Butter Chicken Nachos, 158–59
Chicken Shawarma, 99
Korean BBQ Burritos, 140–41
spices, 9
spinach
Butter Chicken Sauce, 158–59
Corn Chowder, 56–57
Real Green Juice, 41
Sweet & Sour Rice Balls, 186–87
Thai Red Curry Mac n'
Cheese, 116
Spread, Smoky Cheese, 174
squash. See kabocha squash;
zucchini
Stir-Fry, Easy Tofu & Veggie, 128–29
stock, 4
Stone Fruit Galette, 234
strawberries
Mini Strawberry Tarts, 233
Strawberry Cardamom
Scones, 30
sugar, 3–4
sunflower seeds
Everything Bagel Popcorn
Seasoning, 181
Savory Cheese Tart, 177
Sunny Citrus Juice, 41
Sweet & Sour Rice Balls, 186–87
Sweet & Sour Sauce, 186–87
sweet potatoes
My Everyday Roasted Vegetable
Salad, 76–77
Roasted Vegetables, 76
Two Potato Rösti, 26

T

tahini
No-Churn Salted Caramel Tahini
Ice Cream, 226–27
Salted Caramel Tahini
Milkshake, 229
Tahini Caesar Dressing, 200
Tahini Glaze, 31
tarts
Mini Strawberry Tarts, 233
Savory Cheese Tart, 177
tater tots, 6
Breakfast Totchos, 22–23

tempeh
Bacon Kale Pasta, 127
Breakfast Za, 20
The "Creamy" Grilled Cheese, 107
Stuffed Breakfast Danishes,
24–25
Tempeh Bacon Chunks, 100
Tempeh Tuna, 107
Zucchini Carbonara, 146–47
Tex-Mex Mac n' Cheese, 119
Thai Red Curry Mac n' Cheese, 116
thickeners, 4
tofu
Breakfast Totchos, 22–23
Breakfast Za, 20
Charred Corn Salad, 150
Classic Onion Dip, 163
Clubhouse Sandwich, 66–67
Crispy Tofu Fingers, 92
Easy Tofu & Veggie Stir-Fry,
128–29
HFF Famous Bowls, 153
Kabocha Stuffed Shells, 130–31
Mushroom Kimchi Omelet, 18
Stuffed Breakfast Danishes,
24–25
Tofu Ricotta, 130
Tofu Scramble, 14
Tokyo Mix Popcorn Seasoning, 182
Tokyo Street Fries, 185
tomatoes
Bacon Kale Pasta, 127
Blistered Tomatoes, 89
Breakfast Totchos, 22–23
Butter Chicken Sauce, 158–59
Clubhouse Sandwich, 66–67
Easy Brussels Sprouts Pasta,
124–25
Fries & Salad, 80
Sloppy Joe Zucchini Boats, 145
Sundried Tomato, Olive & Chive
Scones, 30
Tortilla Soup, 46–47
tortilla chips
Butter Chicken Nachos, 158–59
Tex-Mex Mac n' Cheese, 119
tortillas
Buffalo Chicken Crunch Wraps,
142–43
Korean BBQ Burritos, 140–41

Red Sauce Enchiladas, 48–49
Tortilla Soup, 46–47
Totchos, Breakfast, 22–23
travel, 236
Tuna, Tempeh, 107

U

Use Up the Hummus Dressing, 201

V

Vanilla Glaze, 212–13
vegetables
for bowls, 86–89
canned or jarred, 8
Easy Tofu & Veggie Stir-Fry,
128–29
fresh, 7–8
My Everyday Roasted Vegetable
Salad, 76–77
Roasted Vegetable Potstickers,
78–79
Roasted Vegetables, 76
See also individual vegetables
vinegars, 9

W

walnuts
Easy Brussels Sprouts Pasta,
124–25
Kabocha Wonton Ravioli with
Miso Butter, 132–33
wraps
Buffalo Chicken Crunch Wraps,
142–43
Spicy Lentil Wrap, 69

Z

zucchini
Ragu Bolognese, 122–23
Red Sauce Enchiladas, 48–49
Sloppy Joe Zucchini Boats, 145
Zucchini Carbonara, 146–47
Zuppa Toscana, 62–63

Portrait Photography on pages III, VIII, 6, 64, 73, 148, 171, 220, 237, 238, and 241 by Vanessa Heins

Ten Speed Press and the Ten Speed Press colophon are registered trademarks of Penguin Random House LLC.

Library of Congress Control Number: 2020947558

Trade Paperback ISBN: 9781984857521

eBook ISBN: 9781984857538

Printed in China

Editor: Kelly Snowden | Project editor: Emma Rudolph |
    Production editor: Zoey Brandt
Designer: Isabelle Gioffredi | Art director: Kelly Booth |
    Production designers: Mari Gill and Faith Hague
Production manager: Dan Myers
Prepress color manager: Jane Chinn
Food stylists: Lauren Toyota and Eugenia Zykova
Prop stylists: Lauren Toyota and Eugenia Zykova
Recipe photography: Lauren Toyota and Eugenia Zykova
Recipe developers: Lauren Toyota and Michelle Li
Copyeditor: Nancy Bailey | Proofreader: Rachel Markowitz |
    Indexer: Ken DellaPenta
Publicist: Lauren Kretzschmar | Marketer: Allison Renzulli and
    Andrea Portanova

10 9 8 7 6 5 4 3 2 1

First Edition